Human Relationships and the Experience of God

Integration Books

STUDIES IN PASTORAL PSYCHOLOGY,
THEOLOGY, AND SPIRITUALITY
Robert J. Wicks, General Editor

also in the series

Human Relationships and the Experience of God

Object Relations and Religion

Michael St. Clair

Integration Books

paulist press/new york/mahwah

Acknowledgments
The Publisher gratefully acknowledges use of excerpts from the following sources: *The Confessions of St. Augustine* by F. J. Sheed (New York:
Sheed and Ward, 1948). Used with permission. *Story of a Soul: The Autobiography of St. Therese of Lisieux* translated by John Clarke (Washington, D.C.: Institute of Carmelite Studies Publications, 1972). Used
with permission.

Library of Congress Cataloging-in-Publication Data

St. Clair, Michael, 1940–
    Human relationships and the experience of God: object relations
and religion/Michael St. Clair.
        p.   cm.—(Integration books)
    Includes bibliographical references and index.
    ISBN 0-8091-3530-2 (pbk.)
    1. Object relations (Psychoanalysis)—Religious aspects—
Christianity.   2. Thérèse, de Lisieux, Saint, 1873–1897.
3. Augustine, Saint, Bishop of Hippo.   4. Psychoanalysis and
religion.   I. Title.   II. Series.
BR110.S714   1994
201'.9—dc20   94-23336
                                                                  CIP

Published by Paulist Press
997 Macarthur Boulevard
Mahwah, New Jersey 07430

Printed and bound in the
United States of America

Contents

To my family: Roslin, Travis and Forrest,
with much love and affection

Foreword

When people are interested in "the spiritual life" they are, **de facto**, saying: "I deeply value **relationships**"—relationships with themselves, others and God. Spirituality and an appreciation of the relationships they have go hand in hand.

Given this, when we turn to contemporary psychology, the school of thought which seems so naturally relevant and supportive to those interested in spiritual maturity is object relations theory. However, since this sophisticated approach to understanding the human person is quite complex in that it stands on the psychological shoulders of a great deal of previous psychoanalytic thought and practice, to mine this theoretical jewel and apply it to further the appreciation of one's own or someone else's spiritual life has been quite difficult for most people. And so, the development of a basic work on object relations theory and the spiritual life has been sorely needed.

With this in mind, Michael St. Clair, the author of the widely-read and respected book **Object Relations and Self Psychology** (Monterey, CA: Brooks Cole, 1986) and a person possessing extensive theological background as well as graduate-level teaching/clinical experience in pastoral counseling and the integration of psychology and religion, was asked to prepare a book on the topic.

The result is a volume that presents not only principles that are understandable and enlightening but also psychological illustrations that offer a clear connection with religious experience. In addition, although St. Clair doesn't skirt the issues and controversies or subtle nuances that are open to question when one attempts an integration of psychology and spirituality from a particular vantage point, first and foremost this book is a practical work. In this regard it serves to be stimulating in one's

1

reflection about the spiritual life: one's own and that of those persons who come to us for guidance.

Exploring the inner world of people is a sensitive and important pursuit. St. Clair respects this. He seems to know the place of knowledge while deeply respecting the mysterious role of grace. As I read this book I was mindful of the warning of the contemplative Thomas Merton that, in our relationship with God, while we must guard our intellect, we must not surrender it. It is a balance between the initiative of God and the responsiveness of the human person; and it is one that this book certainly takes into account.

The developmental and relational "model" that we call object relations theory is presently a group of ideas and findings that can help us better understand our image of God, religious experience, personal integration, and spiritual maturity. To help us see this, the material in this book is expounded by St. Clair in a way in which we can also access some of the main reflections by persons particularly interested in both religion and modern psychology from an object relations orientation (i.e. William Meissner, Ana-Maria Rizzuto, John McDargh). This is particularly helpful because it provides a basis upon which to make judgments regarding further reading in the area if there is a desire to do so.

In essence then, this volume by Michael St. Clair provides a real service to those of us who wish to see in an intelligent way what contributions modern psychology from an object relations perspective can make to our efforts to walk honestly and faithfully with God as we walk with others. And for this I am truly grateful to him for his fine efforts.

Robert J. Wicks
Series Editor

Introduction

Religion is relational and is concerned, in part, with an individual's love and awe and guilt in a relationship with God.

Object relations theory, which analyzes and describes human relations, places relationship at the center of psychological life. Like most psychoanalytic theories, object relations models point out how past interpersonal relationships shape relationships in the present, including the relationship to the sacred. Object relations theory, however, does not deal with the divine object as divine, but simply as another object for study. A faith perspective holds that humans have the capacity to enter into a relationship with the sacred object who is qualitatively different, transcendently different, from human objects. But faith relationships must be congruent with a capacity for human relationships.

Rather than using the term religion, which is not easy to define, this book will refer to religious experience in order to keep a focus on the subjective experiences that individuals have with the object of their belief.[1] Religion, of course, involves many cultural, theological and philosophical aspects that refer to more than subjective spirituality alone, and also includes involvement with external practices and the idea of relationship to a religious community as well—but most of these aspects fall outside the realm of object relations.

In their effort to understand the nature of religion, psychoanalytic researchers have typically approached religious experience as just another area of human activity without according to religion the status of being a special reality or a special mode of knowledge. Believers feel this kind of approach ignores the transcendent realities behind religion and robs religious experiences of the sense of the holy.[2]

3

Freud seemed to dismiss religion as an immature form of neurosis which people must put behind themselves as they mature. Religion for Freud essentially was an illusion and a kind of wish-fulfillment, a creation of the human mind under pressure of infantile needs that had no place in the scientific world of adult rationality.[3]

But psychoanalysis, it must be realized, is a discipline with limits. That is, it is a discipline that can only attend to psychological or subjective realities, such as people's feelings about others, whether those feelings are about parents or God or figments of the imagination. A discipline must confine itself to its proper sphere of competence, and psychoanalysis does not have the means to judge or not judge God's objective existence.[4] A further issue is that Freud's analysis of religion is based narrowly on a conceptual model centered on biological impulses or drives, even though he introduced the richer ideas about object relations upon which later theorists would build.

Psychoanalytic thought has genuine insights into the psychological forces that color religious behavior and experiences. These insights can cast light on the religious experiences of believers and can help us realize how thoroughly religious experience takes place in the context of human psychological life. The concreteness, even messiness, of human life and relationships shapes and influences an individual's religious experience.

The conversation between religion and psychoanalysis has improved as post-Freudian psychoanalytic object relations theories have expanded beyond Freud's early impulse model to clarify the essential relationships that bind people together.[5] Indeed, object relations theory has allowed the psychoanalytic perspective on religious experiences to move well beyond Freudian positions which can now better be seen as limited and culturally embedded.[6]

The task of this book is to make use of insights from psychoanalytic object relations theory to illuminate several different aspects of religious experience. The book is intended for individuals who wish to understand better the connections between religious experiences and psychological life, for counselors who work with religious clients, and for seekers after God who desire a richer sensitivity to the nuances of relationships.

The first chapter presents some of the key ideas of object relations theory along with some of the initial questions that get raised when pairing object relations theory and religious experience. The second chapter expands on the central insight of object relations theory as applied to religion: the origins and development of the representation of God. Chapter three offers some suggestions on the interconnectedness of psychological development and the emergence of religious experiences. Chapter four offers a full case study illustrating some of the ideas of the early chapters.

Any originality in this book lies not in the ideas, but rather in the attempt to bring together in one book some integration of the questions, issues and ideas of modern object relations theory on religious experience. The hope is that readers will not stop with this book but feel inspired to explore further the original rich material of ideas and books that this work tries to present here.

I wish gratefully to acknowledge the generous assistance of several colleagues and friends. John McDargh, William Meissner, Ana-Maria Rizzuto (by phone) were generous with their time and expertise. Padraic O'Hare and Richard Griffin read portions of this manuscript and rendered helpful advice. Robert Wicks and Maria Maggi were most supportive and encouraging. I am very grateful. Any lapses or difficulties are mine alone.

Chapter 1

Object Relations Theory Applied to Religion: Issues and Controversies

What are some of the key ideas of object relations theory? How can these insights be applied to the study of religion? What questions and problems emerge when object relations theory is paired with religion?

A. Objects and Object Relations

Object relations, in psychoanalytic writings, alludes to the nature and origins of interpersonal relationships. An "object" is the other, that is, a person or thing in an individual's external environment which becomes internally or psychologically significant. "Object relations" refers to the feelings and mental images which become associated with dealings with this or that object. Over time early interpersonal experiences cause the build-up of a richness of images[7] which function as psychological structures in the mind and shape how the person's resultant personality relates to the world. Also, the term object relations can be used in a broader sense to refer to the various psychoanalytic theories that discuss the building up of past relationships that shape a person's present relationships.[8]

How did the term "object" ever get used in discussions of human relationships? Like so much else in psychology, it all goes back to Freud. In 1895, in a brief outline of his ideas on instincts,[9] Freud described an infant's hunger and the infant's feelings. He said that the hungry state of the infant made the infant feel a positive attraction toward the wished-for object—or more precisely, the image of the object in the infant's mind.

The object, of course, was the mother's breast which previously had offered warm nurture to the infant. The infant initially relates to a part of the mother, then the mother, then other things and people outside itself.

Thus, object first meant the target of a biological need and got to be used of later psychological needs.[10] Much of the discussion also includes the idea that the object gets taken "inside" the person by means of mental images or representations that also have feelings attached to them. The idea of object relations grew so that the primary motivation of people came to be understood as seeking relationship, not merely seeking satisfaction.

The terms object and object relations carry a lot of theoretical freight; that is, they are used with several related meanings. An infant begins its relationship with the world outside itself by depending on the biological nurture of the mother's breast. Rather rapidly, in the first months and years of life, inner psychological structures are built up within the infant that enable it to relate to people outside itself and also to have a sense of itself as a self. Object relations theory discusses this process of forming intrapsychic structures that are shaped by past relationships and that continue to affect present interpersonal relationships. In other words, current relationships tend to be a new edition of some previous important relationship, a kind of repetition of a relationship from the past.[11]

To illustrate how object relations theorists might think about a person's internal world, let us use a non-clinical example and recall the story of Cinderella.[12] An observer might wonder how a young woman like Cinderella could make the decision to marry the prince after only one wonderful evening with the young man. The object relations theorist seeks to understand her "internal world," and that inner world in this instance might be flooded with feelings of painful emotional deprivation. Cinderella had lost her mother and was perhaps neglected by an inattentive father. Her attempts to protect herself against that pain might have meant that she uses psychological defenses of splitting, whereby she tends to see females as either all good (her fairy godmother) or as all bad (her stepmother and stepsisters). If she felt poorly about herself, it makes sense that she might be attracted to a perceived magical and idealized male, the prince, who showed interest in her and who would whisk her away from her drab world. Obviously a relationship built more on fantasy than realistic knowledge is going to have problems although we never hear the rest of the story, whether the prince and Cinderella get a divorce. The point of object relations is to see how earlier relationships, however rich or troubled, shape how people experience themselves and relate to key persons in their lives.

The psychological relevance of object relations is this: attention to the possible gap between what external observers see occurring between a child and parent or between two adults and what is actually occurring within the inner worlds of the people in the relationship. The relationship may seem to be one between lovers, for example, but the inner reality may be that the seemingly loving man may actually regard the woman as an aspect of his mother. A famous sports hero with a woman on his arm, a woman dressed in mink and lavish jewelry, may regard her as an ostentatious ornament which inflates his self-esteem rather than as another adult with feelings and sensibilities.

Object relations theory is not a systematic school of thought but rather a living body of ideas and notions. Freud had the initial insight and invented some of the terms, but therapists and writers after him have gone in different directions. Freud himself did not fully develop the implications of some of his ideas on object relations. While Freud developed psychoanalysis as a theory of relationships based on biological instincts, later writers have expanded the ideas and put relationships in a central role and clarified people's capacity for intimate relationships. Indeed, there is a general group of theorists and clinicians who are grouped under a heading of object relations theorists but not in any unified or systematized school. Under this broad tent would be included Fairbairn, Winnicott, Guntrip, Klein, and Mahler, as well as the self-psychologist Heinz Kohut who introduced the idea of a selfobject.

The efforts of post-Freudian writers have clarified some of the building blocks of human personality and the means by which helpless infants grow psychologically into adults who can love and relate to other mature adults. Essentially the psychological birthing process involves internalizing or "taking in," as it were, the relationship with external objects to form the internal structures of the personality. To study the human personality means studying the history of the person's relationships with significant people.

Fairbairn and Klein made the initial break away from Freud's biological model by placing relationships at the center of personality. Fairbairn essentially grew disenchanted with the idea of urges and instincts, and said in effect that the human heart is hungry primarily to be in relationship. Fairbairn's psychological model, therefore, is built on a repudiation of Freud's emphasis on drives as basic human motivation.[13]

Fairbairn believed Freud had unnaturally separated psychological energy from the structures that make up personality, and he mocked Freud by suggesting Freudian instincts "bombard" passive psychic structures "much as if an air-raid were in progress." Fairbairn insisted that impulse is not, "so to speak, a kick in the pants administered out of the blue to a surprised, and perhaps somewhat pained, ego."[14] Rather, Fairbairn argued, object relations are a psychical structure in action. Fairbairn worked out a psychology of object relations in which objects taken within oneself as representations become psychic agencies that carry on functions once carried on by real persons outside the self.

Curiously, neither Fairbairn nor Klein devoted much of their attention to religion, although disciples after them would do so.

These extensions of Freud's thought show up in a richer developmental and relational model than Freud's early efforts. The net result of the evolution of ideas in psychoanalysis and object relations theory is emphasis on relationships and not on impulses. This emphasis on relationship allows for a more positive stance toward relation and enables object relations theory to provide—not always systematically—genuine insight into the area of religion.

B. Applications to Religious Experience

1. Image of God

One of the main applications of object relations to religion is the study of the formation of our images of God.

By analogy, what we know about relationships between people can supply insight into how we shape our relationship with God and the sacred, apart from theological questions of grace and a different order of being. As theologians speak of God revealing the divine life and sharing it by means of grace, they reach out for human metaphors and language. Just as St. Paul borrowed terms from the commercial world of his time to express theological realities of redemption, so modern writers express relational themes in terms of an understanding of grace as the divine self-communication in a loving relationship that results in the divine presence and divine indwelling.[15] The area of modern thought that is perhaps best prospected for categories of relationships is psychoanalytic object relations theory which carefully studies the structures and nuances of personal interaction.

The process of becoming a self begins in the family. Not only does the family environment nurture the sense of self in a child by means of images of self and other, there also occurs the development of images of God. In the interpersonal world of very early human relationships the groundwork is laid for the relationship with God. The image of God is a special kind of object representation.[16]

The work of Rizzuto and McDargh[17] points to the development in early childhood of images of the self and also images of God. The contribution of object relations theory is that images of the self and of God take shape in the human context, be it of loving and caring parents, or harsh and limited parents.[18] The child's experiences of relationships that generate images of self and others begin with the parents and end with the child's creation of an inner representation of the divinity long before the child becomes exposed to institutional aspects of religion. Rizzuto insists that the process is not exclusively representational, that is, merely a mental picture. Rather, the process of forming a representation of God involves seeing how the parents pray, how the parents treat each other: so much happens before the fifth or sixth birthday of the child. And the process of forming and reforming the personal image of God is never completed: mature persons re-encounter the God of their childhood in later years at every corner.[19]

The child's sense and image of God is, in a complex way, connected with the child's own parents. The continuity may be direct between the parents as a basis and the God image, or the image of God might be quite opposite so that God in this scenario may be utterly good and protecting, while the parents are regarded as ungiving, mean, and unloving.[20] The opposite, of course, can also be true, so that the parents are idealized and God gets devalued. The essential feature is that family relations form the basis of the God image, but a complex basis. As the child matures into a young person and then an adult, the image of God ordinarily evolves and usually dissociates from parental images and becomes more universal.

The child does not consciously create the image of God out of fantasy, but rather out of the concrete experiences of family prayer, stories, questions asked of parents. Gradually the child is introduced to official and institutional religion, and necessarily there is further reshaping and rethinking of the image of God. Indeed, early religious education does indeed exert an influence here, but to that process of catechesis the child already brings his or her private God. The image or representation of God has all the psychic energy and dynamics of a living person.[21]

Object relations theory is a developmental theory, and its larger view is to depict how human beings relate to others in profoundly different ways at different stages of their development. Hungry infants relate to their mothers differently than considerate adult lovers relate to their loved ones. Relationships and events that take place during development can dramatically shape the individual's religious experience and relationship to God and the sacred. Object relations studies how relationships and events that take place during development can dramatically shape the individual's religious experience and relationship to God and the sacred. The psychological stages of development are successive, that is, later stages build upon the successful resolution of earlier stages. Each human being must move through various phases of challenges that must be worked through and resolved on the path toward becoming a mature and integrated adult. But some individuals have difficulties in some areas of growth and don't always successfully manage to row past difficulties in the stream of life and get stuck or delayed.

Object relations theory, in reflecting on religion, progresses beyond Freud who failed to sufficiently include in his thinking about religion a richer model of development. His theories were limited almost exclusively to the kind of infantile and neurotic conflicts early in development that give rise to adult obsessional and ritualistic practices.

2. Where, Psychologically Speaking, Is Religious Experience Located?

D.W. Winnicott, an early object relations theorist, makes a special contribution to the dialogue between religion and psychoanalysis by suggesting where the psychic location of religious experience is. The issue originates in Freud's idea of religion as an illusion, that is, merely an internal and psychic process. As an illusion, religion, according to Freud, served a defensive purpose to protect against overwhelming feelings of helplessness. For Freud, an illusion might have been necessary to make such helplessness tolerable, that humans "are unable to do without the consolation of the religious illusion, that without it they could not bear the troubles of life and the cruelties of reality. . . ."[22] Freud suggested that humans cannot go on being childish forever, but must grow up and put aside illusions for the sake of having a realistic, that is, scientific and objective, view of the universe.

In contrast to Freud, Winnicott sought to bridge the split between public and private worlds, the subjective and the objective. He suggested that there is a "third area of human living," "an intermediate area of *experience*."[23] This psychological space is a product of the interaction of the inner world of the individual with the objective environment in which we all live. This intermediate reality is interpersonal, right from its very beginning in the interaction between mother and infant.[24]

The origin of "illusory" experience comes early in the developmental experience of the child, from the baby's trust in the mother experienced over a long period. Winnicott coined the phrase "transitional objects" for those soft toys or blankets that served as a bridge between the physical presence of the mother and a mature capacity to hold a comforting image of her in the mind while getting along independently of her. Thus, by clutching a teddy bear or a mother's old silk stocking, the toddler is able psychically to evoke the comforting presence of his mother when she is physically absent. The use of the soft toys, so called transitional objects, indicate acts of fantasy or imagination by which children view the world in ways that blur the sharp distinction adults make between internal and external reality. The result is an intermediate area of experience that offers a safe transition between the objective and subjective realms and by so doing unites them. The use of these transitional objects demonstrates a human capacity for illusory experience that is simultaneously subjective and objective, a middle ground that is neither purely external reality nor purely inner or psychic hallucination.[25]

Relevant for our study here, Winnicott expanded and enriched the meaning of illusion by finding this same kind of illusory experience inherent in art and religion. These realms are the realm of symbolism, the capacity for which begins with the use of transitional objects. Winnicott says that the toddler's soft blanket symbolizes or stands for the mother's soothing breast, but the blanket is not the mother or her breast, and that is equally important.[26] Symbolism seems to take place in this intermediate realm of experience that Winnicott terms illusionary. Thus real external objects can become the means for expressing subjective significances. The symbolic quality of such objects participates in the realm of illusion, where there is a blend of external reality and subjective attributions that result in meaning. Meissner finds that religious experience involves this compounding of subjective and objective, where there can be a compounding that is not merely subjective nor exclusively objective. Religious symbols, such as the crucifix, bread and wine, and the star of David, become vehicles for the expression

of meaning and value not merely from their physical characteristics but also from the attribution of significance to the object
by the believer.[27]

Winnicott's elegant solution helps us to realize that this
realm of transitional phenomena is thus also the realm of play,
art, religion and creativity—so many quintessential human experiences. There is, of course, a progression in the cognitive
and psychic mechanisms which elaborate the adult experiences
in this realm. Indeed, it is in this realm where the human potential may find its greatest expression in the religious and faith
experience.

This realm of illusion was Winnicott's psychological attempt to leap the subject-object gap, but it remains for theologians and philosophers to further elaborate the epistemological
issues involved. Clearly faith moves beyond images of God and
assertions of trust. Faith asserts something, or, more correctly,
Someone, beyond trust. This is the creative moment in the "illusion" of faith.[28]

3. Which God Does Object Relations Theory Talk About?

Those who apply object relations theory to religious experience can broadly be placed in two groups, the psychologists
of religion and the religious psychologists.[29] The psychologists
of religion seek to understand and explain religious phenomena. Generally these affirm a kind of methodological neutrality,[30] keep boundaries of their psychological discipline and do
not make those kinds of statements that are more "appropriate
for philosophers and theologians."[31] On the other end of the
spectrum are the religious psychologists who have a commit-
ment to religion, make use of psychological concepts, have
sympathy with religious beliefs and appreciate the adaptive
role of religion.

The first group, the psychologists of religion, would be
careful to use only psychological language—not theological
language or the language of faith—and consequently would define God in terms of psychological reality. "God, psychologically speaking, is an illusory transitional object."[32] They inves-

tigate the subjective and intrapsychic experiences of people, especially those experiences that involve objects of religious belief. They are not interested in moving to questions of affirming or rejecting the object of believers' faith.

On the other hand, religious psychologists are sympathetic to religious experiences and beliefs. Object relations concepts add to their language, and open up ideas about the "real" object "behind" the representation of God. They might argue that the deep human yearning to be in relationship points in the direction of a God who satisfies that universal need and who has objective (that is, not merely psychological) existence.[33]

Harry Guntrip, who played an important role in circulating the ideas of the British school of object relations, adopts this pro-religious stance when he says that object relations puts the nature of personal relationships in the very center of human inquiry about the meaning of existence. Since religion is pre-eminently an experience of personal relationship, religion extends the "personal" interpretation of experience to the nth degree, to embrace both humans and their universe in one meaningful whole. Development involves personal relationships at every stage. Part of maturity, reaching the full potential of person in relationship, is also to be in relation to a personal God.[34]

Guntrip finds that "integration, maturity, mental health and religious experience are all closely related."[35] The basis for this is the primacy of the need for good personal relationships: ". . . religion is *about* the human's innate need to find good object-relationships in which to live his life."[36]

Another pro-religious psychologist is Moshe Spero who is interested in the nature of the reality of the image of God. Spero affirms the parallel dimensions of relationship among persons and between persons and God.[37] Spero, appreciating the illumination offered by object relations theory on the adaptive and developmental aspects of belief, is especially interested in the question of what "degree of reality to attribute to the thing-that-lies-behind the god representation."[38] Spero is concerned about the objective reality called God, the real object "out there," and feels that the psychological approach alone has still not given us access to the transcendental entity that is to be found beyond the early mother-child matrix or oedipal triangle.[39]

Also pro-religious is the psychoanalyst Leavy who also focuses on the epistemological issue of God—what exists on its own and is not just a part of private experience or something subjectively invented. For those working in counseling with patients who assert that God has somehow been present to them, Leavy's advice is not to regard such accounts as illusions or delusions. Rather, Leavy argues for "leaving open the possibility that the transcendent otherness that religious persons claim to approach is as real as they claim it to be . . . recognizing that there are more things in heaven and earth than are dreamt of in our philosophy."[40]

But some tension still can exist here, because believers, while using the language drawn from object relations, need to be alert to the limits of psychoanalysis and the different methodology of theology. Attfield argues for God's existence based on religious experience, alleging that experience is always experience of *something*.[41]

The significance of these issues is this: Many psychoanalytically trained psychologists work with patients who have religious experiences. Counselors need to appreciate the role and importance that religious experiences have for the patients. The issue, then, is to accept and value the religious experiences of people and to help discern healthy from troubled religious experiences.

4. *Can Religion Serve as a Positive and Integrative Force in an Individual's Life?*

A religiously oriented psychologist might outline a functional role for religion, that religious faith helps troubled individuals adapt and cope with life.[42] Harry Guntrip is perhaps the most senior object relations theorist to assert the positive role of religion: ". . . that religion is *about* the human being's innate need to find good object-relationships in which to live his life."[43] While affirming that "integration, maturity, mental health and religious experience are all closely related," Guntrip also acknowledges that Freud "did show that there are neurotic forms of religion which are an essentially infantile longing for a lost Mummy and Daddy."[44]

Thus, religion can serve an integrative function in a person's life and can contribute to psychic equilibrium. If the growing child has had early developmental experiences that foster a sense of trust, the child feels safe to enter into various relationships. Part of the process of forming a sense of self and one's identity comes from being in these various relationships, among which relationships is one with the supreme Other or the supreme Subject. Positive images of God developed during the earliest years in pre-oedipal and oedipal struggles with self-becoming contribute to the young person's growth in the experience of love and trust, and that person is likely to experience the world outside of oneself as positive and benevolent.

Faith and religious functions build on the basic human capacities of the individual.[45] Positive relationships foster trust, just as trust fosters positive relationships. A person's religious experience rests not only in concepts, but also deep within a person's bones, as it were, connected with family history and all past relationships. A healthy religion orients the individual positively in the universe, helps the individual deal with a universe that is benevolent, as opposed to a universe that is colored with rage and fear, with no sources of hope or comfort.

Religion can be a mature, healthy expression of meaning that supports the individual. Religion plays its role in the maintenance of the self by helping to hold the self together and avoid psychological fragmentation.[46] In the face of the difficulties of life, a person's images of God and the person's relationship to God serve a crucial psychic function of assisting in providing for a coherent sense of self in a world that might seem chaotic at times. Further, relationships with God and a community can help the individual move outside and beyond a self-centered view of the world and transcend the boundaries of the self.

Chapter 2

The Internal Image of God

Introduction

Central to the believer's religious experience is the relationship to God. The actual beloved and loving God, however, is not seen or heard or touched, but is powerfully present psychologically to the believer.[47] How can we think about and discuss the believer's relationship to the living God with all the varying feelings of guilt, doubt or joy?

Psychoanalytic object relations theory, which is interested in the key people in an individual's life, can cast light on a person's relationship with God by considering that special relationship in terms similar to the other significant persons in the individual's life. This is done by using the idea of a subjective image or representation of God that the individual has developed, similar to other inner representations or images. The consideration of these images provides some understanding of how different people have very different kinds of relationship with God, ranging from a comforting, loving relationship to no relationship at all. A person might fear God as a harsh distortion of an Old Testament Father-God, or feel close to God as Gentle Lover. Psychoanalytic object relations theory also helps in a discussion of the uses of and changes in the God representation during life, and especially at moments of crisis.

Ana-Maria Rizzuto and the Image of God

Foremost, after Freud, among those psychoanalysts looking at how individuals relate to God has been Ana-Maria Rizzuto. Rizzuto began her interest in looking at religion through the eyes of her discipline in 1963 when she was asked to teach a course in a seminary on the psychological foundations of belief. During the teaching of the course she grappled with those elements in a child's formative years that facilitated and interfered with belief in God.[48]

Rizzuto's Method of Discovery

Inspired by Freud's insights into the role of the parents in the formation of the representation of God, she began a research project with patients admitted to a private psychiatric hospital. Twenty patients were studied, ten men and ten women. The goal of her project was to study the possible origins of the individual's private representation of God and its subsequent elaborations.

Rizzuto took her basic hypothesis from Freud who had connected the individual's "father in the flesh" with God; that is, Freud claimed that we create our own gods on the basis of early relationships shaped in childhood. His insight was simple: the nature and quality of one's important relationships tend to be shaped on the basis of the memory-traces of the early prototypes of childhood relationships.[49] Rizzuto's hypothesis, accordingly, was that there were parallels in the subjects' childhood relationship with parents and their images of God and relationship to God. Rizzuto maintains that people's dealings with their God are as complex as their dealings with other people—be it in early childhood or any other age—dealings that are imperfect, ambiguous, dynamic, and by their very nature have potential for both integrating and fragmenting the person's psychic experience.

To collect data from her subjects, Rizzuto had each one fill out a detailed questionnaire and then she interviewed each to gain a comprehensive life history. Seeking to understand her subjects thoroughly, Rizzuto asked them to talk about themselves at the different stages of their growth, about their relationships, about their conflicts and problems. Her end goal was to be able to make a complex assessment and come to a clinical interpretation of the quality of each subject's relationships in those private and subjective areas of experience which do not lend themselves easily to statistical analysis.[50]

It was not easy, however, for Rizzuto to gain a clear profile of each subject's God as felt and perceived by the subject as well as the complex relations the subject had previously, and still hoped to have, with God. Rizzuto also had to understand the objective sources the patient had used to form his image of God and how the images were influenced by teachings received from religious institutions. In short, human experience is rich, but the inner world of psychic reality is even more complex.

The Formation of the Representation of God

Rizzuto investigates the relational experiences that an individual has, starting with the parents and ending with the child's creation of an image of divinity. The process is not exclusively representational, that is, merely a mental picture. Rather, the process of forming a representation of God encompasses complex psychic, maturational and relational changes which affect the overall development of the individual and result in the person having a relationship to a God that has all the psychic potentials of a living person.

As indicated in chapter one, object relations theorists assume that in the earliest relationships individuals form subjective images of the object with whom they are in relation. The individual's early emotional relationships color and shape how the person forms an image of God and relates to God.

These images or representations are not static entities. The pressure of living pushes all of us to work and rework over and over consciously and unconsciously the memories of those we encountered during childhood. It is out of this matrix of facts and fantasies, wishes, hopes and fears in the interactions with those incredible beings called parents that the image of God is concocted. Indeed, the process is never over.[51]

The Nature of the God Representation

Rizzuto focused on the formation of an individual's private representation of God during childhood and its modifications and uses during the entire course of life. She calls this process of formation the "Birth of the Living God." What is born is a new original representation which has elements that serve to soothe and comfort and provide inspiration and courage far beyond that inspired by the actual parents on whom the image may have been based originally.

Rizzuto concluded that the components of the God representation come from varied sources, wider than merely images of one's father or mother. As to the developmental stages from which images are drawn, Rizzuto says that the images and experiences from the earliest years, before the oedipal struggles, seem to play a key role. Indeed, she concludes that formation of the image of God does not depend upon the oedipal conflict, but rather that the image of God results from a process of image-formation arising during an emotional relationship with a key person or several key figures. Indeed, factors from many different development levels converge to form the image of the complex reality that we name God.[52]

The process is something like this. A three year old pre-oedipal child, for example, has great curiosity and wants to know the why of everything. She is especially interested in the causes of things. Why do trees move? Where does the wind come from? How are babies made? How were mommy and daddy made? Her ceaseless chaining of causes—animistic notions of causality—inevitably leads her to think of a superior being. The idea of God suits a child well because her parents and adults are already in her mind superior beings of great size and power. The child easily moves to an anthropomorphic understanding of God as a powerful being like her parents, only greater. There is curiosity about God's behind and genitals, his toilet habits and how God can see her all the time. Afire with intellectual curiosity, the child creates God amidst a rich mix of managing her own aggrandized parental representations, her own grandiosity, her need for affection and love, her fear of separation and loss of love, her sexual urges and sexual fantasizing about babies and body parts.[53]

In short, the representation of God each person produces is a compound image that results from all sorts of contributing factors, feelings, relationships, the psychic situation prior to the oedipal period and during the oedipal complex, the characteristics of the parents, the predicaments of the child with each of his parents and siblings.

The Private (Representational) God and the God
of Organized Religion

However the child alone does not create a God. Watching her parents pray, attending church and encountering official ritual, hearing adults talk about God, all further shape and expand the image of God that the child develops. But children bring their own God, the one each has assembled, to this official religion, which encounter really only occurs **AFTER** the image of God has been formed. Now the God of official religion and the God of the child face each other and, through the child's reshaping and rethinking, there is a blending and a second birth of God. This process of reshaping and rethinking is of crucial import for catechists: if they wish to understand the progress of children's refining their notion of God—a process which goes on throughout life—it is desirable to have some knowledge of the private God the individual child brings to the catechetical process because, most likely, formal religious education adds little to the representation of God that has already been formed. As Rizzuto succinctly says: "No child arrives at the house of God without his pet God under his arm."[54]

The Idea of God Versus the Representation of God

The idea of God and the God representation differ on both the conceptual and the emotional level. The concept of God is usually at a conscious level of thinking, the God of the scholars and theologians, the God which may not move us emotionally. The God representation, on the other hand, is made up of images, feelings and memories from early childhood. This God, from its multiple causes, has an emotional claim on us that the more conscious, conceptual God doesn't. John McDargh speaks of the "sophisticated theologian who had thought his notions of God had been properly and critically demythologized [and who] is amazed to discover in a moment of personal crisis that he was spontaneously evoking the God of his childhood bedtime prayer."[55]

The God representation, because of its experiential origins in the perhaps antagonistic or too sexualized relationships with parents, has a psychic aliveness because it originates and gets elaborated in the actual experience of the person's life. Generally speaking, the integration of the conceptual God with the representational God requires considerable soul searching, self-scrutiny, and internal re-elaboration of the representation.

In short, the representation of God supplies a sense of the psychic reality of God, that is, the sense of God as real, existing, alive and interacting with the believer. Belief makes God a truly unique "object," the only relevant object who has not undergone and cannot undergo reality testing. Religious believers feel the relationship to be real and intense. They do not experience God as a symbol or a sign but as a living being.[56]

Rizzuto, as a psychoanalyst, can only speak of the psychic reality of God, the psychological experience of God; she is not a philosopher or theologian whose realm is the life of faith and the reality of God's existence, the areas of faith and grace.

Development and the God Representation

A basic thesis of Rizzuto is that no child brought up in normal circumstances passes through the oedipal period without forming a rudimentary God representation, which may become part of the individual's active religious life or may simply lie latent and inactive in the unconscious.

Throughout the life cycle of the person, there are possible transformations and changes in the God representation of the person. The further developmental stages of the individual may leave that representation untouched (as he or she continues to revise parent and self-representations). Unless the God representation is revised to keep pace with ordinary changes in self-representation, the God representation can soon become out of touch with the growing self-image and consequently could be experienced as ridiculous or irrelevant or, on the contrary, threatening or dangerous.[57] But this is the theme of the next chapter.

Every catechist knows how some sophisticated adults can have an infantile childish religion that simply has not kept up with their emotional and intellectual development.

Categories of Relationship

Rizzuto suggests that most human beings, in their adult religious experiences, can be located in one of the following categories: A) having a God with whom they relate in varied ways; B) wondering whether to believe or not in a God whom they are not sure exists; C) amazed, angered or quietly surprised to see others deeply invested in a God who does not interest them; D) struggling with a demanding, harsh God they would like to get rid of if they were not convinced of his existence and power. To summarize these positions, one might say: I have a God, I might have a God, I do not have a God, I have a God but I wish I did not.[58]

Rizzuto does not oversimplify people's religious experiences. She suggests that there are potentially a number of different ways of relating to God. She says it is possible to describe and categorize different types of "gods" or "god-images" which people create for themselves in the same way in which we describe and categorize different types of interpersonal relations as oedipal, clinging, or passive-aggressive.

Case Study of Fiorella Domenico[59]

Rizzuto provides several lengthy case studies, one of which is summarized here. Fiorella Domenico was an attractive and kind woman of Italian background. She was the second of five children. Her father was a hard worker and clearly the head of the household. Fiorella described herself as an adolescent as quite "happy-go-lucky." When she was eighteen, her mother introduced her to a young man with whom she quickly fell in love. Shortly the two young people married. Fiorella had two children, and much of her adult life passed without major events. She felt things had gone well, and she enjoyed her life.

But when she was thirty-eight years old her father died, and two years later her mother. Her son left to be married the following year, and six years later her daughter also left to be married. Shortly after her daughter's wedding came a frightening experience for Fiorella when her husband had an acute kidney stone attack, and she feared that he was dying.

It was at this period in her life that she began getting anxious and fearful. She began to feel phobic at church, anxious about being in the front pews. With her husband in such intense pain she was frightened that she might lose him, and subsequently she became so claustrophobic that she felt unable to attend church. Her phobias took the form of a fear that people were closing in on her and that she was suffocating. She was increasingly feeling panic and frightened of death so that she sought psychiatric help. This is how she came to the attention of Dr. Rizzuto.

Rizzuto understood Fiorella's composite representation of God as originating mainly from her interactions with her father. God, for her, is a living being, who protects and watches over his children as a good father does.

Rizzuto matched the words that Fiorella used in describing God with the words she used in describing her father. Although there were some characteristics of God that came also from her relationships to her mother, it was very clear that her father was the most loved person in her life—even after she had been married for twenty years—and that her representation of God had many of her father's characteristics.

Rizzuto found that the God representation underwent the re-elaboration of the oedipal experience and subsequent latency period—that is, Fiorella formed a harmonious and idealized representation of her parents and herself under the need to be good and to share in a good relationship with the protecting parental figure. Rizzuto felt that Fiorella's development of her God representation stopped at latency. She did not undergo a crisis of doubt or disbelief or re-evaluate the parental authority figures, but basically accepted their morality and ideals. Fiorella has the image of a loving and comforting God, but also perhaps an image that has stopped growing. She never seems to have needed to leave her parents behind, but agreed to stay at home and never had to explore the world at large. She was genuinely loved and cared for— with the consequence that this positive experience did not pressure her to move on to other objects.

Fiorella reduced the universe to the size of her household, as Rizzuto says. God is one more safe, domestic figure. It was only the threat of various separations—from husband and daughter that began the experience of anxiety and claustrophobia, especially in church. Rizzuto hypothesizes that Fiorella experienced the unimaginable threat that she could lose her husband and this challenged potentially how she saw God as watching over her and protecting her. She was not in touch with her anger toward God or abandoning objects, so hers was a reaction of anxiety and phobia. She assumed that her God representation failed her, the God who watched over her and protected her. Her fear of dying or being left alone caused anger and dismay which she displaced onto the church which she subsequently was not able to go near. These defenses allowed her to keep intact her self-image as a good, loving person, and God could remain a loving object, and thus her psychic equilibrium was preserved, but at a cost.

In summary, with regard to Fiorella's belief in God, she is in the first category, that is, of having a God whose existence is not questioned, a God with whom she has a very positive relationship. Her representation of God seems to be from the developmental level of libidinal object constancy—that is, the latency period with an idealizing love for a safe and protective oedipal object.

Fiorella's representation draws its characteristics from her paternal representation primarily, but there are some components from her maternal representation. Rizzuto feels her God representation is a direct continuation of parental representations and idealized parents, a complex representation of images, concepts and emotions. Rizzuto believes it is the kind of representation that seems to coincide with the type of representation used by a child of the latency period—that is, free of contradictions, or intellectual questioning.

Fiorella represses sexual and aggressive wishes, which allows her to obtain great satisfaction from her relation to the God of her official Catholic faith who was protective, loving and stern enough to converge without major conflict with her oedipal paternal representation.

On a psychiatric level, Rizzuto diagnoses Fiorella as suffering from acute anxiety neurosis and claustrophobia. Her anxiety comes from the fear of abandonment and loss of love, but she has established effective obsessive defenses.

Rizzuto's Achievement

Although Rizzuto stands on Freud's theoretical shoulders, as it were, she reaches beyond him. Her understanding of the God representation differs from Freud's representational fossil that is frozen at some developmental level. Rizzuto understands that the representation of God is a genuine creation of an "imaginary" being, a new original representation which may have the varied components that serve to soothe and comfort, provide inspiration and courage far beyond that inspired by the actual parents. Her reasoning provides an explanation for belief in God by people who are neither so infantile nor so regressed as to make us suspect they are reacting to some childhood trauma or clinging to some father or mother god.[60]

The originality of Rizzuto is her emphasis on the powerful reality of object representations. Drawing on Winnicott's illusory, transitional objects which are creations of our minds, Rizzuto is able to demonstrate how understanding the representations of God illuminates the analysis of religious experience. The importance, however, of Rizzuto's contribution is that using the resources of psychoanalytic technique and theory, she helps us understand how God functions in the inner world of the individual with all the psychic potentialities of a living person.

A possible flaw in the methodology work of Rizzuto, however, is that her material is largely drawn from the ranks of troubled individuals. She tends not to draw upon well-integrated individuals and her adherence to strict psychoanalytic discipline does not allow her to see as clearly as she might the positive role of religion in fully mature individuals.

Further Empirical Research

Rizzuto's work has sparked, as well as been a part of, a major reworking and thinking of the psychoanalytic approach to religious experience. She welcomes empirical, well-thought through studies that will refine the conceptual application of object relations theory to the study of religion.[61]

An example of just such research that sets out to examine

some of Rizzuto's formulations about the development and use of God representations is the work of Marilyn and William Saur.[62] These researchers interviewed ten adults who had been psychoanalyzed. The researchers questioned the subjects about their religious experiences. The data seemed to confirm Rizzuto's concepts about the nature, origin and functions of the God representation.

Rizzuto's work has especially ignited considerable discussion among those who are working on issues of faith and the relationship with God. Perhaps foremost among these scholars is John McDargh who uses psychoanalytic object relations theory in the dialogue with theology. He finds that the contribution of psychoanalytic object relations theory, especially the work of Rizzuto, has two related aspects: it offers a coherent psychological account of the human side of faith and, secondly, draws into consideration a key element in religious experience, the object of faith as God.[63] The importance of images, McDargh explains, is that faith is a reasoning of the heart by means of personal images. Individuals use images of the transcendent in order to sustain the integrative activity of faith, and individuals draw upon the images of God that arise uniquely in the pre-oedipal and oedipal struggles for self-becoming.[64] Like others who work from a pro-religious stance, McDargh sees that religion contributes to psychic functioning and equilibration.[65]

McDargh sees faith as a way of being in relationship with what is ultimately real and trustworthy in the universe. Faith involves meaning, and the meaning, using the insights of object relations theorists, is to be in relationship. McDargh is interested in the pre-verbal, pre-conceptual experiences that are the foundation of the human inclination to search for a divine object. For him faith "is descriptive of a total reaction to life as it comes to us, a relationship taken to our ultimate environment."[66] The orthodox psychoanalyst would probably see this as too mystical, too opaque, language that is not the standard psychoanalytic terminology.[67]

Another aspect of the faith experience is the on-going search for the relationship or experience that transforms.

Building upon the theoretical work of Rizzuto, Edward P. Shafranske[68] calls some object-representations transforming objects because they originate and become internalized during early childhood experiences of transformation. Shafranske is interested in applying the idea of the transforming object to the God-representation in order to build a conceptual model of change and human transformation, especially in the realm of religious experience. Transformation experiences in infancy are indelibly etched into the deep psychic structure of an individual's consciousness. When a special form of the God-representation is seen as a transformational object, Shafranske implies that new insight is gained into certain kinds of profound individual religious experiences, especially experiences of the transformation of the self.

Chapter 3

The Influence of Early
Psychological Development on the
Adult Experience of God

Introduction

Early psychological development contributes to the organization and shaping of adult religious experiences.

Just as object relations theory serves for reflecting upon
the psychological structures (the inner representations of oneself and others) that shape relationships, object relations theory
can also illuminate those religious experiences that involve the
adult's relationship with the divine object.[69]

The Jesuit psychiatrist, W.W. Meissner, has applied object
relations theory and other classic psychoanalytic concepts to
religion to illustrate the interplay of psychological development with religious experiences. He contends that unfinished
development tasks and residues of childhood development
shape and color adult religious experience.[70] Meissner suggests
several "modes" of religious experience that reflect the organizing influence of different levels of childhood development.
No one has attempted this before and the modes or schema are
somewhat sketchy. The modes are primarily descriptive and do
not evaluate the religious quality of the experience, nor is there
any suggestion that God changes or develops in the way the
human subject does. Meissner's notion of religion is also
broader than Rizzuto's more narrow focus on the relationship
with God. The modes progress from residues of earliest development coloring adult religious experiences to later development issues and residues.

The task of this chapter is twofold. Because it is during

early development that the inner psychological structures of self and object representations become established, an investigation of these early relationships with parents and other key figures illuminates the individual's adult relationship with the special object, God. This chapter considers the parallels between human interpersonal relations and the relationships between the individual and God. Because of the complexities and mysteries of religious experience the effort here is still preliminary and suggestive as it is not yet possible to arrive at a nice neat schema. This chapter will make reference to the work of Meissner but not follow him in all particulars.

Religious experiences have varying qualities and intensities. Why is this? The psychological suggestion offered here is that adequate development in infancy and childhood provides the pre-conditions for mature adult religious experiences, and conversely, a residue of some early developmental conflict or unresolved disturbance can cause some forms of troubled or immature religious experiences in adulthood.[71] What this means is that spiritual and religious experiences, however complex and only partially articulated, are intertwined with psychological realities and need to be seen and understood within the context of human development and cannot be isolated from the full range of psychological life.[72]

The focal point for discussion is the God representation.[73] Chapter Two presented some of the dynamics that went into the unconscious formation of the God representation. The current chapter seeks to reflect upon early life conditions and the successive stages of development of the God representation which contribute to the adult's God representation and adult religious experiences.

Psychological Development

Development implies that a human being is not born with adult capacities, but that there are successive phases of building up and organizing an individual's personality and relational abilities. Further growth depends on the successful resolution of the conflicts of the previous phase.[74] Thus when the developmental process is considered as a whole, the personality is a composite of its successive developmental achievements and their more or less successful integration as well as any residual deficits and archaic remnants from the unresolved struggles of some early phase of development. It is these archaic remnants and the return of these deficits that can not only cause psychological problems in adulthood but also cause the individual's religious experiences to be immature or even neurotic—from the viewpoint of psychology, not faith and theology.[75]

The successive phases of development of an individual's object relations, with the concomitant development of the God representation, seem relevant to the shaping of the individual's religious experiences and the individual's relationship to God—from a psychological point of view. The development of the God representation is linked to the development of object relations. The ultimate goal here is to try to understand and get insight into a person's adult religious experiences by means of these developmental processes.

Development takes place not merely during several successive phases, but on several different tracks at each phase. Psychoanalytic theories, for example, consider how human development takes place simultaneously on a narcissistic line of development, that is, how well an individual can put aside attention to oneself in order to invest emotionally in another person. Can a young teenage mother, amidst her own developmental needs, be as invested in another, her baby, as capably as a woman who has completed more of her psychological development? Can a teenage father be as responsible to and for others as a man who is further along the social and developmental track?

Rather than getting absorbed by other lines of development, we shall focus primarily on the development of object relations since that developmental area has a special relevance for the shaping and coloring of religious experiences.

Development of Object Relations and the God Representation

The direction of growth in object relations is inextricably linked with the quality of parental care, especially the care provided by the mother. In its earliest period, the infant is absolutely dependent on the mother, but gradually this dependence changes toward a relative dependence and then increasingly toward independence with the capacity to be in a mutual relationship with another.[76] It is essential, of course, to recall that development involves an overlapping of stages, of progress forward, then falling back in order to move forward again.

The God representation reflects and parallels the development of human relationships. More specifically, the characteristics of the God representation form at the key developmental moments when the child is forming basic object representations, and Rizzuto links the sources of the representation primarily to the parents, who provide most of the characteristics of the representation. The research task is to reconstruct the early life conditions and traumas which may have contributed to the child's elaboration of a particular God representation that emerges in his or her adult religious experiences.[77]

The relationship with parents provides the early basis for representations of God. The connection, however, between these representations varies. There can be direct continuity between the characteristics of parents and the characteristics of the God representation. Or these can be directly opposed, so that for example God might be loving and protecting, while the real parents are rejecting and ungiving. Or there can be a rich mix of good and bad qualities in both the God representation and the parental representations.[78]

1. Earliest Stage: Psychological Fusion with the Mother Along with Lack of Differentiation[79]

Earliest development is a state of lack of differentiation; that is, the infant has no sense of any distinction between self and non-self during the first weeks of life. Indeed, the infant does not yet have the mental capacity to realize that it is in a state of absolute dependence on another, the nurturing parent, but the infant does have body memories and pre-verbal experiences.

The infant's early intrapsychic *experience* is one of psychological fusion with the mother, a state in which the self-representation is fused with the representation of the mother.

An essential element is the experience of mirroring on the part of the mother where she provides a loving and caring presence for the child by her admiration, hugs and kisses. The earliest object representations, accordingly, are of the mother. On a primitive emotional level, the infant experiences the self, as far as the self has developed, as fused with the mother and with images of oneness with the mother.[80]

This early period sees the building up and consolidation of early "good" self-representations and "good" representations of objects. That is, when the infant has pleasurable experiences of feeding or being held, the good feelings get associated with images of the self, and those good feelings are also connected with, perhaps, an image of the mother's face or breast. Frustrating experiences likewise build up "bad" representations of the self and objects with painful and angry feelings. Such negative feelings might be represented in this anachronistic way, if the infant had words: "I am hungry and I feel terrible and I am furious at my mother's depriving, absent breast."[81]

The infant likely has a feeling of omnipotence that comes from the seemingly magical fulfillment of its needs without any effort—if there really is a good parent providing whatever care is necessary. As the representations form, part of the earliest self-representation is of a grandiose and omnipotent self in relation to an idealized object.[82]

If the infant's earliest object-representation is of an idealized parental image or object, then it follows, as Rizzuto suggests, that the prevailing characteristics of the God-representation share in the characteristics of the parental representations. Developmentally the first God representation is made from the real or wished-for good mother of a small child. This God is a kind and loving presence who is always present.[83]

Rizzuto gives an example of an adult whose God representation derives almost exclusively from her mother. This individual, as a young child, lost her father and then at about four or five was traumatized in her relationship with her actual mother. Because of the absence of a father, she was unable to use characteristics from a father to form her God representation. The need for a caring mother took precedence. As a child other adults offered her compassionate help, and so she continued to want an idealized mother who would treat her like a child. Consequently, as an adult she sought substitute mothers who would continue this kind of care. Her God representation was created from her traumatic experiences with her own mother. Her adult preoccupation was one of finding a mothering object, and her God fulfills primarily the maternal functions—a caring presence.[84] A person with a God representation largely formed from maternal qualities might make statements about God in the following way: God "provides for my needs," has "a complete understanding of how I felt," has "ability to fulfill my needs," fills me with "love, peace, assurance," etc.[85] Of course, if the individual's father has been experienced this way, then the God representation is formed more from the paternal representation.

The earliest actual religious experiences of childhood, say perhaps at two or three years of age, are derivative and intertwined with the real mother. The child easily imagines God, and these early images of God have almost exclusively characteristics of the child's own parents, characteristics of protection and authority. Whatever childhood religious practices the child has, perhaps saying bedtime prayers, seeing parents with bowed heads praying or going to church, etc., will be mixed in the child's imagination with fantasy and fusion. The family is the model for religious experiences, with the sense of authority and protection.[86] Ambivalence toward the parents is reflected in ambivalence toward God. If the mother is protective and loving, then there is the building up of images of a loving and kind God. Conversely, as the mother punishes the child or is harsh, the child easily attaches images to her of fear and avoidance, and likely the child also attaches fearful and awe-inspiring images to the God representation. The basic trust that the child experiences with the mother would serve as a foundation for a later trusting faith in a loving God. If positive images of mother predominate, there is the concomitant likelihood of positive possibilities of religious experience.

Adult Religious Experience

Adult modes of experiencing God, shaped or colored by these earliest of developmental experiences, are somewhat paradoxical: in psychological terms, they seem to be of a primitive or deeply regressive state, yet may also have the most profound of religious experiences.[87] In this psychological condition there is no separation of the self-representation from the object-representation, with the consequence that the psychological state is one of fusion and symbiosis. This condition or state has usually been called one of primary narcissism in which the inchoate self is absorbed in an experience of unconditional omnipotence.

Because there is no differentiation between self and other or even between one's inner psychic realm and what is outside the self (the world of the non-self), the kind of cognition that the person has, specific to faith, is a pre-conceptual and pre-linguistic acceptance of the experiences offered to consciousness. On a relational level there is present the experience of basic trust that exists in the symbiotic union of mother and infant. To illustrate this from the experience of St. Therese (cf. Chapter Four), the mystic uses the idea of a drop of water in the sea to suggest the sense of merger with her Beloved, even to the temporary loss of her own boundaries. Such a sense is not unusual in mysticism, and even Freud used the expression "oceanic" experience for this kind of religious experience.[88]

This mode of religious experience has a quality of merger wherein boundaries between the self-representation and God (or God representation) remain diffuse. The self of the initial stage of development is inchoate, undifferentiated or even fragmented, and consequently religious experience in this earliest mode is either of mystical union or of a very disturbed, regressive kind, such as a psychotic level with delusion of omnipotence and Godlike grandiosity.

If the religious experience is of profound mystical union, it involves a loss of boundaries, a diffusion of self and an absorption into the Godhead or into the universe. This unitive experience might be compared, as many mystical writers have done, to two lovers who experience a temporary dissolution of the self and a seeming absorption into the beloved object. In theological terms, of course, God does not lose himself—we can only speak of the psychological aspects of the human experience. There is the further issue, on a psychological level, that images of lovers are much more likely to be oedipal issues, that is, later and more mature developmental issues. The erotic imagery of the Song of Songs is suggestive of a mode of religious experience shaped by different developmental structures.

On an unhealthy level, a state of negative psychological regression, could also resemble a kind of religious psychosis, a state of hallucination. Such an individual may have religious experiences that are more troubled or, perhaps, not drawn from a conventional religious tradition.

2. Stage of Early Psychological Differentiation

The early phases of differentiation overlap other subphases of separation and individuation.[89] The young child passes through, as it were, a kind of psychological birth as an individual, with the achievement of separate functioning in the presence of and with the emotional availability of the mother. Differentiation will manifest itself in such behavior as the infant's early pushing away from the parent in the first year and issues of toilet training in the second and third year, with increasing indications of independence during this period.

This stage of development starts when the self-representation differentiates from the object-representations; that is, the infant begins to clearly delineate self from the non-self world. The stage ends with the integration of "good" and "bad" self-representations into an integrated self-concept, and the integration of "good" and "bad" object-representations into whole object-representations.

While this stage marks the differentiation of the self, the self is not yet fully cohesive or integrated. But the child is less reliant on external objects (parents) for internal functioning, even though the child continues to depend on external objects for help in key functions such as the regulation of impulses and self-esteem, for example. In Kohutian terms, parents serve as self-objects; that is, they play an important role in fostering the child's self-esteem and well-being by "mirroring" (showing joyful appreciation of the child) and allowing the child to idealize them (when the child attributes to them unrealistic status and power). The risk of psychological fragmentation gradually recedes as the growing self increases its cohesiveness and integration.

This stage could also be considered a stage of early triangulation, an early aspect of the oedipal period—that is, the growing awareness of the presence of a third person (in classical theory, the father) and the growing awareness that the world of relationships is not merely one of me-and-mom-alone. The child needs to grapple with the issue of a third person in the world of intimate relationships and integrate the feelings of being a part of a threesome—or even more, if there are siblings and grandparents and uncles and aunts.

The God representation, at this early stage of the oedipal period, may be a compound representation of the parents, having both father and mother characteristics, but ordinarily the mother—if she is the primary caretaker—still dominates as a source of characteristics that become part of the God representation.[90] Rizzuto offers examples of individuals whose God representation derives largely from the parents "as a couple,"[91] wherein the individual seems to perceive the parents as a couple. The God representation will likely be of a protective presence with some characteristics from both parents.

But if major trauma should interfere at an early stage, the child who is already very aware of the presence of a caring and powerful father may not be able to integrate the experiences and will thus carry a parallel God representation, one made of the maternal traits and another of paternal traits. When the child's self-awareness increases and becomes infatuated with life outside the self and the family, strong desires for power can emerge. The child's father provides a model for imitation in desire for power and self-aggrandizement. Power attributed to the father soon gains entry into the God representation, as well as into the greatly idealized self-representation.[92]

As the child grows cognitively, the child learns things are made by people, and so develops early notions of anthropomorphic causality. The child asks questions about where things come from. "The answer that God made the world or the sky can be envisioned only in anthropomorphic terms—God is a person who is big enough, powerful enough, to make very large things."[93]

Adult Religious Experiences

The key issue of adult religious experiences here is differentiation and what flows from the developmental process of differentiation.[94] On the object relations level of development, the self representation differentiates from the object representation. The cohesiveness of the still-emerging self depends on the idealized other because a self that is prone to regressive fragmentation counters by the connection to an idealized, omnipotent other. Accordingly, the quality of the faith experience is one of utter dependence on and awe of the omnipotence of the God representation.

Even though there is a sense of difference between the self and the other, the experience is one of dependence on an idealized other. The emerging experience of inner and outer worlds connects with the narcissistic line of development at this phase. Characteristic is the dependence of the inner grandiose self on an idealized, omnipotent other. This dependence on the other (the parental image or representation) is absolute and essential for the sustaining of the very fragile emerging self. Indeed, the cohesion of the self requires this idealization of the parental image and a dependence on that idealized omnipotent parent. Psychologically, any threat or hint of separation from that idealized figure causes concern and perhaps even anxiety at the possible fragmentation or dissolution of the self.

The God representation that evolves at this early stage, accordingly, is very much in terms of the perfect, omnipotent idealized image. Religious feelings are in line with this: utter dependence and awe at the omnipotence of the Godhead. Religious experiences characteristic of this mode are permeated with feelings of submission and, perhaps, conflicts between autonomy and dependence. For example, after a period of intense infatuation with God and religious practices, because of a conversion experience, the individual may feel the need for autonomy and declare a kind of independence from God that echoes the experiences of the early practicing period as described by Mahler.

In some adults, with characteristics from this stage of development, it is likely that there are superstitious impulses to placate the awesome power of the omnipotent, omniscient God by ritual and magical practices. Scruples can occur, with hesitations about the right way to act because of religious uncertainty or fear of offending the figure who is of such power and authority. The pious individual greatly fears separation because of what might happen to the self. There is a kind of magical thought process permeating religious experience, and this compulsive, magical quality colors the believer's relationship to the image of God.

Meissner suggests that religious experience tends to be strongly colored by elements of animism, based on the operation of projective mechanisms similar to those described by Freud's account of demonic and spirit illusions. God is all good, the devil is all evil. Images of God may be pre-anthropomorphic, for example a kind of pananimistic sense of God as a presence and force in everything rather than any sense of God as personal or warmly approachable. The images of God could also be anthropomorphic, but not so much cognitively as emotionally, as a child absolutely dependent on a maternal figure. Cognition and affect are still somewhat confused, while the feeling quality of the experience usually predominates over the rational and logical. God is felt, more than thought of, in animistic and magical terms as the omnipotent and omniscient presence or force. To depend on such an omnipotent and idealized God creates conflicted feelings that might get resolved by masochistic submission and superstitious placation.

Religious practice consequently follows this sense of God's awesomeness. God is to be placated by superstitious and magical ritual: God is not a person but an awesome force and power that the self needs and needs to try to control.

This and the next modality seem to be the one area that Freud described in his obsessive compulsive neurosis theory of religion.

3. Integration of Self-Representations and Object-Representations and the Development of Higher-Level Psychological Structures

This intermediate developmental period solidifies the emergence of the self as a cohesive individual. Good and bad images of the self coalesce into a whole self system, while good and bad representations of the object are integrated so that the child now has a more realistic representation of the mother as a whole person with both good and bad qualities. This stage, lasting approximately from the end of the third year through the sixth year, overlaps Mahler's practicing, rapprochement and object constancy sub-phases; that is, the separation-individuation processes are being completed.

Key personality structures are consolidated, such as the ego and superego, with the superego beginning to function as an independent intrapsychic structure, although at early levels the superego involves harsh, punitive images. Psychological defenses are developed. Cognitive abilities are also maturing, and these thinking skills contribute to integrating self and object images in a more realistic view of the world. By now the child is well established in the social world of pre-school or kindergarten or first grade.

The child imagines God in terms of the most formidable human beings he knows, his parent. God representations at this stage initially make use of characteristics of both parents, but increasingly more of the father gets included in the God representation, especially if the father is the more aggressive or stern parent. Rizzuto, however, believes that, contrary to Freud, no individual uses only the representation of the father in forming the God representation, even though that God representation by now has predominantly paternal characteristics.[95]

(The feminine characteristics of God have not yet been fully worked out by theologians, but there is an effort to expand the metaphors by which we speak of the divine mystery.[96] Unquestionably male metaphors have predominated in the Judeo-Christian tradition. It is most interesting that perhaps depth psychology is supportive of feminist theologians investigating female imagery of God in the Bible and in tradition—or at least helping theorists understand better why there was such exclusive reliance on male imagery for God.)

Oedipal issues seem important because of the intense feelings involved. The God representation that had already included aspects of both parents may become sexualized. If oedipal conflicts are resolved and the parental representation is desexualized and exalted into a Godhead, the individual[97] may have a most pleasant and satisfying relationship with God. Sometimes scary or difficult aspects of a parent can be split off, and these negative qualities can be attributed to the devil. When the father is an overwhelming figure in the child's life, the God representation is all the more likely to be based on paternal characteristics.[98]

If a child's father occupies an overly powerful position in the family and is overpowering for the child, the child's God representation might take on feared and despised characteristics. Rizzuto mentions an adult, David Miller, whose God representation was vivid, but observes that Miller was a non-believer who did not want anything to do with such a frightening God.[99]

The child continues to work out the distinction between God and parents. The child gains a more realistic view of the parents as human beings, with their individuality and limits.

Adult Religious Experiences

These key developmental advances can shape adult religious experience.[100] Perhaps the central development that serves as the lens for experience is the cohesiveness of the self. This means that there is a better delineation between the inner and outer worlds which allows for better distinguishing between the individual's inner processes and external realities. The individual's religious belief is accordingly less magical, more involved with cognition and rational understanding, but there is still a tendency to continue to rely on feelings, that is, belief based on a trusted authority outside oneself, such as the church or tradition, rather than a reliance on one's own judgment or experience or logic.

Religious thinking about God and the origins of things is

usually mythic, usually anthropomorphic, and tending to be literal, concrete and one-dimensional. Emotionally and cognitively there is not yet the capacity or interest to resolve in a sophisticated way competing myths or sources of information. If there is conflict in religious belief, the individual feels more comfortable in relying on an authority than on personal judgment and logic. The cohesive self can better distinguish between internal processes and external reality, with the consequence being that religious practice is less magical. The individual, preoccupied with law and order, can have concerns about punishment for transgressions and concerns about rectitude and obsessive ritual performance.

As to the evolution of the image of God, it is less maternal than the preceding mode and more paternal, reflecting the child's anxieties toward the oedipal father. As Freud showed in two classical case studies of obsession[101] it is not surprising that a child can displace anxieties and ambivalence toward the father onto an exalted father-God. Even though the anxieties of the oedipal period can get projected onto the divine object, religion is not co-extensive with obsessive rituals or ritualized ceremonial.

4. *Latency and Puberty: Consolidation and Integration*

This end-of-childhood stage involves the final integration of the superego. The young person also continues to solidify an ego identity and self-concept that has continuity and direction.[102] In general the individual, through interactions and experiences with "real" people in the external world, continues to reshape the inner world in such a way that there is a more realistic, balanced and mature view of oneself and others.

Essentially the individual now has adequate internal resources to face the external world of difficulty and challenge. The internal world shapes the person's perception of the external one and experience of the external world reshapes the inner representations into a more harmonious whole. Distorted images of parents gradually get reshaped into a more realistic perception and understanding of their values and frailties.[103]

During the elementary school years the child becomes

aware of the distinction between God and parents. Children of latency age (from about seven to ten) tend to view God as more universal, and these children begin to dissociate the image of father from the image of God. But God is anthropomorphic—a magnified human, but the individual's ideas of God are progressing in the direction of a more spiritualized Godhead.[104]

Adult Religious Experiences

Meissner believes that most adult religious behavior falls under this modality.[105]

Religious experience is marked by the presence of a consolidated superego. This essentially means that with a mature conscience, an individual can possess and express ideals and values. The locus of authority moves within the individual rather than merely existing external to the self. The individual can experience anxiety or guilt because of not attaining the goals of one's internalized ideals and values.

Because of involvement in the social world of family, friends and school, the individual has attained the cognitive skills to deal with a more complex, multi-dimensional reality. The individual increasingly relies on personal judgment and a growing capacity to select and evaluate authoritative positions, even though the individual may fall back on an external authority to buttress personal judgment because of some lingering uncertainty. Relational skills mature so that the individual is more comfortable and experienced in differentiating between the subjective and objective, and multiple levels of meaning. There might be prejudice against the beliefs of others, however.

Because of the mature cognitive skills, a growing ability to see distinctions and make evaluations, the individual can appreciate symbolic meanings—but there is still a sense of unevenness and lack of a full confident and personal religious synthesis. The individual can have a coherent belief system and be in affiliation with a church that buttresses and supports the belief system. Increasingly the individual can go either in the direction of casting off institutional notions and authority in order to take fuller personal responsibility for values and beliefs, or more and more be in subordination to an external institution and ideology which seems to offer simple resolutions to complex issues. Meissner believes it is a fertile area of study to see the interaction between the personal and institutional here.[106]

5. *Adolescence and Young Adulthood*

In adolescence individuals attempt to see their parents with new eyes, and intense doubts can be present as the young person tries to deal with the meaning of life. If the parent representation has been co-mingled with the God representation, the youngster may abandon God as a way of getting distance from parents and parental values. The parent representation can be tested, as Rizzuto suggests, under the disguised name of God while the young person searches for meaning and God in a philosophical or religious quest. But ordinarily, by the end of adolescence, the God representation has acquired the basic traits that are to last for life, though some new additions and transformations are still possible. At this point the God representation is complex and made from the many exchanges between the individual and the parents.[107]

The adolescent has a more personalized image of God. The adolescent begins to internalize notions, make them more in tune with adolescent needs, affective needs. The highly personalized God of the individual may not be well integrated with the God as described by organized religion when adolescents sometimes attribute to God qualities they would like to find in their friends. Boys tend to idealize God in ways that adolescent girls do not; adolescent girls tend to emphasize loving relational qualities in God.[108]

Each life crisis offers an opportunity to revise the God representation or leave it untouched. Any such intense life moment as the birth of children, serious illness, death of a parent, can provide the situation for possible revisions in one's self-image. One other period relevant to the history of the individual's God representation is puberty with the onset of capacity for abstract thought and emerging intellectual skills that allow for the expansion of the *concept* of God beyond the limits of the adolescent's own *representation* of God. The end of adolescence with pressing life issues, such as marriage and the work world, can also push the growing young adult to integrate a more cohesive and unified self-representation.[109] As the self-representation changes because of pressures of the adult world, there also occur concomitant changes in object-representations and the God representation.

Adult Religious Experiences

What is the religious experience of someone with full psychological development? The normal individual is at the highest level of integration and capable of the fullest mutual relationship with another, with the least distortion. The individual has mature psychological skills that imply the ascendancy of the ego and its control over drives. The individual is able to manage anxiety, and danger no longer arises from within the individual's own inner world (such as the fear of psychological disintegration or fragmentation), but rather from extrinsic concerns (real dangers external to oneself). Also, on the developmental level, is the integration of healthy narcissism which enables the individual to have a full measure of wisdom, empathy, humor and creativity.[110]

A person of mature spiritual and psychological life is able to embrace, affirm and somehow resolve the tensions of life, to integrate them in a more balanced faith orientation and faith existence. Such an individual can look upon religious belief systems and their traditions in increasingly realistic terms which enables the individual to tolerate inherent tensions and ambiguities. Such an individual can affirm and hold to the beliefs, ritual symbols and ceremonial of a religious community in all their relativity, partiality, limitations and particularity.[111] At the same time this knowing through faith is able to acknowledge the existence and validity of other faith traditions adhered to by different persons and different cultures.

With a mature capacity for mutual loving, some individuals can have spiritual experiences of special graces and mystical gifts. It is probable that only a few individuals attain such an inner life of lucid simplicity, a kind of inner harmony, which paradoxically seems to be more fully and profoundly human. Meissner suggests that the love of God in these individuals

seems wholly unself-conscious, stripped of infantile residues.[112] In brief, in their relationship with God and fellow humans they bring the capacity for profoundly meaningful object
relations which are characterized by a selfless love and acceptance of others. Another generation freely used the term saints
for such remarkable persons.

While psychology tends to use language of regression for
profound religious experience of God, perhaps the careful
scrutiny of saints would show that such terms as primitive regression is inappropriate to the description of intense religious
experiences, especially the experience of God. It may be that
we need to re-evaluate the higher reaches of spiritual attain-
ment and see it in terms of an enlargement and intensification
of the fullness of unremitting object love.[113] Maslow's[114] psychological language, such as peak experiences, may not have
been too far off with his appreciation of spiritual experiences,
for such expression can embrace the intensely human and intensely spiritual, especially those experiences with the least
amount of primitive or negative regression, the temporary loss
of boundaries in acts of love with the beloved.

Adulthood and the Life Cycle

Human psychological development does not stop with the
successful formation of an intact personality that can relate mu-
tually with others. Adults, of course, go through continuing ad-
aptation and changes in life, often with markers of development
that are external, such as career, marriage, retirement. As an
individual grows through the life cycle, there can be further
attainments of wisdom, the ability to articulate their vision and
ideals. Also needing to be noted is the growing body of
work drawing attention to issues of gender difference in
development.[115]

Not all aging is inevitable progression. But in the midst of
the life cycle, from a religious and faith point of view, the person can experience God profoundly, however distorted and
limited that experience may be from a psychological perspective. All that can be offered here is an attempt to show how
psychology thinks about the organization of some of these religious experiences.

Conclusion

Other scholars, like James Fowler, have suggested different levels of faith development, but his methodology and categories are primarily oriented toward the content of faith and are primarily theological and he has not made use of psychoanalytic notions of relationship.[116] Freud's application of psychoanalytic insights to religion fell short, in part because he focused on a narrow range of troubled religious activities that reflected limited developmental influences. Post-Freudian models, such as object relations theory, articulate a richer developmental model and consequently provide richer insights into human spirituality.

Chapter 4

Case Studies of Two Contrasting Saints

The task in this chapter is to place two individuals of extraordinary faith and spirituality within a psychological context. By the use of object relations theory this chapter will attempt to see the impact of their psychological development on their religious life and experience of God.

The goal of this exercise is not to explain away the religious genius of St. Augustine or St. Therese of Lisieux but rather to draw on the language and concepts of object relations to aid in thinking about the shaping experiences of early life that can distort or enhance religious experiences. Neither saint is a psychiatric patient, but rather both were chosen here because of their extraordinary religious lives and influence, and because the reader may have had some passing familiarity with their lives and writings. Also, the "cases" were chosen for didactic purposes because some elements are quite overt and can readily be applied to contemporary individuals encountered in current spiritual direction, pastoral counseling or retreat work.

In lieu of interviews with these saints we have their contrasting autobiographical works. Both wrote dramatic and articulate accounts of themselves. Augustine's personal revelations in his *Confessions*[117] can be mined for some insight into his conflicts and perhaps how he managed to adapt and resolve those conflicts or how those conflicts continued to handicap him. The *Confessions*, ostensibly written to show how a sinner found the path to God, is an unique study of the self by one of history's great minds and personalities. It is at once an act of piety, a process of therapy and a genuine confession.

St. Therese, in about every way imaginable, contrasts with Augustine. She led a very different life and wrote a very different kind of autobiography.[118] Indeed, St. Therese's *Story of a*

Soul, while reflecting the pious conventions of late nineteenth century rural France, offers a simple account of her growth and a particularly interesting demonstration of some of the developmental ideas of the last chapter. Nevertheless, despite the seeming opposite extremes, Therese and Augustine have strong similarities: their faith, their contributions to the life of believers, their human strengths as people of their times.

The lessons for us are the parallels between their developmental issues and their spiritual journeys.

St. Augustine of Hippo (354–430)

Augustine was born in Tagaste, in Roman North Africa, to Monica who was a fervent Christian, and to Patricius, a pagan civil servant. The religious difference of the parents led to some conflict which affected Augustine's development. His father was a willful and hot-headed man who wanted his son to be a pagan like himself whereas Monica is depicted by Augustine as having a great determination that her son should be a Christian. (I.11, 12, 17)

A hint of Augustine's narcissistic qualities and self-centeredness is highlighted by the fact that in the whole of his autobiography, he makes only one off-hand reference to a brother but doesn't name this younger brother (Navigius) and does not mention his sister at all. (IX.11)

As a youth Augustine loved playing: "I loved the vanity of victory." He enjoyed praise, and could fly into a rage, and had the desire "to be thought the best." He was a young man of strong feelings who wanted "to love and be loved," who was aware of beautiful bodies and his own strong sexual feelings, but when he looked back at his youth when he was writing his *Confessions* he spoke harshly of these feelings as "evil desires ... abominable sins. ..." (I.10; II.2, 5)

Both parents recognized the extraordinary gifts of their first son, and indeed he was "regarded as a youth of much promise." They made sacrifices for the education necessary for his career. Augustine was sent off to school in Madaura, a nearby city. At sixteen he was idle while his parents gathered

funds to send him to the university at Carthage, the great North
African city. (I.16; II.3)

When he finally arrived at the university at Carthage, "a
cauldron of illicit loves leapt and boiled about me. I was not
yet in love, but I was in love with the idea of love. . . ." In his
adolescence he conveys the impression of great sexual activity
and speaks of "the filth of unclean desire." He also was caught
up with a love of the plays on stage. But he continued in "the
study of the law, in which I meant to excel—and the less honest
I was, the more famous I should be. . . . By this time I was a
leader in the School of Rhetoric and I . . . was arrogant and
swollen with importance. . . ." He began to see law as less use-
ful than rhetoric and eloquence, an arena in which he had am-
bition to make a name for himself. (III.1–4)

During this period, one day at the baths, his father rejoiced
at Augustine's signs of puberty because it meant a kind of im-
mortality through grandchildren. Monica's reaction to her
son's arrival at puberty was different. "She was stricken with a
holy fear. And though I was as not yet baptized, she was in ter-
ror of my walking in the crooked ways. . . . I still remember her
anxiety and how earnestly she urged upon me not to sin with
women. . . ." Monica advised her son toward chastity so that a
wife would not prove an obstacle to his career. (II.3; III.3)

Augustine's references to his father Patricius are few. Of
his father, Augustine says he was "violent," but he did not beat
his wife as was common at the time. Monica also "bore his acts
of unfaithfulness quietly." Augustine tempers criticism of his
father with the reflection that "my father was still only a catechumen, and a new catechumen at that" (IX.9; II.3)

In contrast to his father, Augustine's mother plays a central
role in his life. She was a "great comfort" to him and her death
was a wound. When she died he says "my soul was wounded
and my very life torn asunder, for it had been one life made of
hers and mine together." Indeed, he blames himself for "too
much of earthly affection," meaning that it was too human and
not grace-filled, as opposed to incestuous as some have tried to
maintain. (IX.12, 13)

Monica was a pious woman who gave alms, prayed night
and day, and "who let no day pass without attending . . .

church." Many of her prayers were for her son. He is aware of his mother's "too earthly affection" for him. "For she loved to have me with her, as is the way of mothers but far more than most mothers. . . ." In general she is idealized throughout the *Confessions*. (V.8, 9)

He did study the Christian Scriptures, but they "seemed to me unworthy to be compared with the majesty of Cicero." With his later Christian insight, he looks back and describes himself at this time as "swollen with pride, but to myself I seemed a very big man." He was troubled with philosophical questions, and was restless to find answers. He makes frequent references in his autobiography to his mother weeping and praying to God for him because of his immoral ways. (III.5)

Augustine's father died when Augustine was seventeen. Augustine continued on with his studies, and from his nineteenth to twenty-eighth year he became a teacher of rhetoric in the town where he was born, but he also says, "I was astray myself and led others astray, was deceived and deceived others. . . . I pursued the emptiness of popular glory and the applause of spectators." He says he "was all hot for honors, money, marriage." During these years he lived with a woman, and was faithful to her even though they were unmarried, but he never gives her name. He did have a son by her, Adeodatus. It perhaps was part of his motivation to defy his mother; it is noteworthy that after the death of his father, the "winning of the oedipal triangle,"[119] that Augustine did two things his pious Christian mother would most strongly object to: get a concubine and embrace the Manichaean heresy. (IV.1, 2; VI.6; IX.6)

He also became exceedingly close friends with a man who had been a fellow student, "a friendship that had grown sweeter to me than all the sweetness of the life I knew." "I thought of my soul and his soul as one soul in two bodies." This friend fell sick and converted to Christianity and soon died. Augustine suffered a deep loss and became aware of how unhappy his life was, a continuous theme of the *Confessions*. (IV.4, 6)

Augustine left Tagaste and came to Carthage. He continued his career, wrote books which he dedicated to Hiereus, a Roman orator, whom Augustine had never seen but admired because of "the fame of his learning. . . . But he pleased me

mainly because he pleased others ... that orator whom I
so admired was the kind of man that I ... wished myself to
be." (IV.14)

When Augustine was twenty-nine the Manichaean bishop
Faustus came to Carthage. Augustine was a Manichaean for
nine years and very much hoped that Faustus would respond to
some of his questions. Upset when it became clear that Faustus
could not answer his questions, Augustine lost enthusiasm for
Manichaeism and the "effort and determination to make progress in the sect simply fell away...." Part of his difficulties with
the sect involved not understanding how incorruptible spirit
could be mixed with corruptible flesh, how the Savior's nature
could "possibly be born of the Virgin Mary, unless it were mingled with her flesh. And I could not see how that which I had
thus figured to myself could be mingled and not defiled. Thus I
feared to believe the Word made flesh lest I be forced to believe the Word [was] defiled by the flesh." (V.6, 7, 10)

Augustine set out for Rome to teach the same subjects he
had taught in Carthage. His mother "was in dreadful grief at my
going and followed me right to the seacoast. There she clung to
me passionately, determined that I should either go back home
with her or take her to Rome with me, but I deceived her. . . .
Thus I lied to my mother, and such a mother; and so got away
from her. . . . She would not return home without me. . . . That
night I stole away without her: she remained praying and weeping." (V.8)

From Rome he went to Milan to be a professor of rhetoric.
At Milan he met Bishop Ambrose, who as a "man of God received me as a father. I came to love him, not at first as a teacher
of the truth ... but for his kindness towards me." Augustine
began to see that the Scriptures could be understood in figura-
tive ways whereas he had taken them literally. He began to see
that the Christian "faith, for which I had thought nothing could
be said in the face of the Manichaean objections, could be main-
tained on reasonable grounds." He finally decided to become
"a catechumen in the Catholic Church—the church of my parents. . . ." (V.13, 14)

By this time his mother had joined him. Augustine found
Ambrose's celibacy "a heavy burden." Nevertheless he

yearned to pour out to Ambrose all the questions and agitations boiling up within him. Augustine began to see that even though man is created by God in his own image (Genesis 1:26), that did not mean that God was in the shape of the human body or had limbs and parts. His conversion process continued, and "I found myself preferring the Catholic doctrine." (VI.3, 4, 5, 11)

What stopped him was the "thought that I should be impossibly miserable if I had to forego the embraces of a woman." He felt he was incapable of giving up the pleasures of sex—that he was "bound by this need of the flesh, and dragged with me the chain of its poisonous delight . . . stuck so fast in the grip of that particular lust as to affirm whenever we talked of it that I could not possibly lead a single life." (VI.11, 12)

He made a proposal of marriage, and his mother "played a great part" in arranging this marriage because she wanted him to be baptized. The young woman was still two years below the marriageable age. The woman ". . . with whom I had lived so long was torn from my side as a hindrance to my forthcoming marriage. My heart which had held her very dear was broken and wounded and shed blood. She had gone back to Africa, swearing that she would never know another man, and left with me the natural son I had of her. But I in my unhappiness could not, for all my manhood, imitate her resolve. I was unable to bear the delay of two years which must pass before I was to get the girl I had asked for in marriage. In fact it was not really marriage that I wanted. I was simply a slave to lust. So I took another woman, not of course as a wife." But things "grew more hopeless," and he "became more wretched." (VI.13, 15, 16)

Augustine, however, began to experience some inner resolution, and he could later pray in thanksgiving to God: "Lord, with a gentle and most merciful hand You worked upon my heart and rectified it . . . You were near me, I sighed and You heard me, I was wavering uncertainly and You guided me. . . ." Augustine often contrasts his unhappiness with the satisfaction he found in God: "At that time my soul was in misery, and you pricked the soreness of its wound, that leaving all things it might return to You, who are over all and without whom all would return to nothing." (VI.5, 6)

He wrestled with the ideas of evil and corruptibility. He believed God was incorruptible and unchangeable, but how could the good God create what was corruptible and change-able? How could humans, made by God, willingly choose evil? He struggled with these ideas. He sought to understand the or-igin of evil. "Such thoughts I revolved in my unhappy heart, which was further burdened and gnawed at by the fear that I should die without having found the truth." He increasingly began to realize the limits and inadequacy of his understanding of God. "O God my aid . . . with all the ebb and flow of my thought You did not let me be carried away . . . Your substance was unchangeable, and that You cared for men. . . . But though I knew it not, You were listening. . . . You knew what I was suffering and no man knew it. . . . You are my true joy." "O eternal truth and true love and beloved eternity! Thou art my God, I sigh to Thee by day and night." (VII.2, 5, 7, 10)

Part of Augustine's insight was the goodness of things. "And it became clear to me that corruptible things are good. . . ." God was not evil, nor were God's creations evil. Evil, rather, was a "swerving of the will . . . towards lower things and away from You, O God." "I marvelled to find that at least I loved You and not some phantom instead of You; yet I did not stably enjoy my God, but was ravished to You by Your beauty. . . ." (VII.12, 16, 17)

He turned to the writings of St. Paul. In 386 he underwent an emotional conversion experience. He was still struggling with his vanities and his mistresses. "When my most searching scrutiny had drawn up all my vileness from the secret depths of my soul . . . a mighty storm arose in me, bringing a mighty rain of tears." He withdrew to a garden one day with his friend Alypius. In great torment, he flung himself under a fig tree and wept. "And suddenly I heard a voice from some nearby house, a boy's voice or a girl's voice, I do not know: but it was a sort of sing-song, repeated again and again, 'Take and read, take and read.' . . . Damming back the flood of my tears I arose, inter-preting the incident as quite certainly a divine command to open my book of Scripture and read the passage at which I should open. . . . I snatched it up, opened it and in silence read the passage upon which my eyes first fell: *Not in rioting and drunkenness, not in chambering and impurities, not in contention and envy: but put ye on the Lord Jesus Christ and make not provision for the flesh in its concupiscences.* I had no wish to read further, and no need. For in that instant, with the very ending of the sentence, it was as though a light of utter confidence shone in all my heart, and all the darkness of uncertainty vanished away. . . . Then we went into my mother and told her, to her great joy." (VIII.12)

He withdrew into the country and there were days of quiet given over to reflection, prayer and reading the Scriptures. He concentrated his effort as a catechumen with Alypius, another catechumen who was also his "heart's brother." Monica was also there: "[M]y mother also was with us, a woman in sex, with the faith of a man, with the serenity of great age, the love of a mother, the piety of a Christian." Augustine soon withdrew from his teaching position and was baptized. (IX.4)

Soon after his baptism Augustine and his entourage decided to return to Africa. On the trip home they paused at Ostia where Monica died at fifty-six years of age. A few days before her death Augustine and she were looking out the window and shared an ecstatic experience which Augustine describes in erotic terms that are used either of union with a lover or with God. "[S]he and I stood alone leaning in a window, which looked inwards to the garden. . . . And our conversation had brought us to this point, that any pleasure whatsoever of the bodily senses, in any brightness whatsoever of corporeal light, seemed to us not worthy of comparison with the pleasure of that eternal Light, not worthy even of mention. Rising as our love flamed upward towards that Selfsame, we passed in review the various levels of bodily things, up to the heavens themselves. . . . And higher still we soared, thinking in our minds and speaking and marveling at Your works: and so we came to our own souls, and went beyond them to come at last to that region of richness unending. . . . And while we were thus talking of His Wisdom and panting for it, with all the effort of our heart we did for one instant attain to touch it; then sighing, and leaving the first fruits of our spirit bound to it, we returned to the sound of our own tongue . . . we two had but now reached forth and in a flash of the mind attained to touch the eternal Wisdom which abides over all: and if this could continue, and all other visions so different be quite taken away, and this one should so ravish and absorb and wrap the beholder in inward joys that his life should eternally be such as that one moment of understanding for which we had been sighing. . . . You know, O Lord, that on that day when we talked of these things the world with all its delights seemed cheap to us in comparison with what we talked of." (**IX**.10)

Within five days Monica fell ill to a fever and shortly after died. Augustine returned to Africa and began an active life as a cleric and became bishop of Hippo in 396. Ten years after his conversion he wrote his *Confessions*. He wrote prolifically, preached and defended the Church. He achieved great fame, engaged in many controversies and struggles. "[T]he writing was now in Your service." (**IX**.4, 11)

Reflections on Augustine

Although there is an extensive literature on the psychology of Augustine as revealed through his autobiography,[120] the concern here is how his early development, specifically his object relationships, set a tone for his relationship with God.

a. Most commentators are in agreement on the extraordinary close relationship that Augustine had with his mother. The question is not that he had close ties but what the significance of this was for his inner religious life.

A central aspect of development for males is to differentiate from the mother. Early infantile development occurs in relationship to another person. Part of the task for very young boys in the formation of identity is to differentiate from their mothers, to deal with the reality that they are not the same as their mothers. Mothers (and fathers) must walk a delicate line between being emotionally depriving and being overly protective. Some mothers obtain gratification from the experience of oneness with their infant or because the infant is an extension of themselves.[121] If Monica was ambitious, it was clear that through her son she gained considerable achievement in a world where women had no direct access to fame or fortune.

Through the evidence from the *Confessions* we can see

some of Monica's over-involvement with Augustine as a young man, a quality of intrusiveness, such that he felt he must sneak away from her when he left Africa. Some of the efforts to differentiate and get some distance from such a mother can resemble rebelliousness. It is accordingly not unreasonable to interpret the young Augustine's sexual involvement with a woman and his involvement with Manichaeism, in part, as proceeding from his need to be different from the kind of person that Monica so much wanted him to be.

Eventually Augustine resolved his conflict (separate identity versus fusion), so that he was able to be close and affectionate with his mother and she became part of his household and was near him during his conversion to Christianity. Indeed, when he was returning to Africa shortly after his conversion, he and Monica shared a kind of ecstatic moment—he felt at peace with her and with his relationship with God. The gradual rapprochement with Monica enabled him to come to terms with "her" God, the Christian God. Somehow the rapprochement with his mother coincided with his openness to, and passionate involvement with, God. Somehow the death of Monica seems to have freed him, in part, to follow a celibate path along the road to faith.

. b. Who is Augustine's God? The mature Augustine, as a well-educated man and a man rich in relationships, clearly was in relation to a rich and complex God. Written when he was a mature man, the *Confessions* contains abundant references to an overwhelming and powerful God, an omnipresent God. The *Confessions*, a dialogue between himself, God and the reader in direct and emotional language, reveals a person of introspective genius and feminine sensitivity. The positive side of his extraordinary close relationship with his mother was the development of these human skills of introspection and relationships—and his faith.

On the basis of the terms and phrases Augustine uses to describe God, it is possible to make some cautious statements about Augustine's representation of God. It seems that early in his youth he linked God with his mother—and in trying to resist her over-involvement, it was easy to resist God whom he linked with his mother. Finally coming to terms with her was

paralleled with his coming to terms with God, a surrendering
to the all encompassing God, a God that at times may have
seemed as all encompassing as an overly fond mother. Just as
she loved him so much (V.8, 9), so Augustine feels a passion to
love and praise God: "And man desires to praise Thee. . . . Thou
does so excite him that to praise Thee is his joy. For Thou has
made us for Thyself and our hearts are restless till they rest in
Thee." (I.1) Indeed, it has been said that Augustine's prayerful
soliloquies to God in the *Confessions* might "equally well describe the infant's experience of the good-enough mother
merged with her adoring child."[122]

The ecstatic language that Augustine uses implies a God-
representation drawn predominantly from characteristics
linked with his mother rather than from his father. Elements of
Augustine's relentless mother Monica are clearly discernible in
the God of Augustine, reflecting the positive side of his relationship with Monica.[123] Presumably Monica was a devoted
mother to the infant Augustine, a mother who served as a powerful figure who held the infant internally and externally and
served as a self-object. That is, a key service of a self-object or
a parent is to reflect back to the infant that the infant is special
and loved. Augustine's prayerful addresses to God in the *Confessions* portray an overwhelming loving and idealized God.

Time and again Augustine links God with his mother:
"Thus for my sustenance and my delight I had woman's milk:
yet it was not my mother or my nurses who stored their breasts
for me: it was Yourself, using them to give me the food of my
infancy . . . by Your gift that those who suckled me willed to
give me what You had given them: for it was by the love im-
planted in them by You that they gave so willingly that milk
which by Your gift flowed in the breasts." (I.6)

The intensity of the relationship with Monica carried over
into his relationship with God, with the same blurring of boundaries. To some extent, the image of God is shaped by images
of his mother. He speaks of her warnings about chastity when
addressing God: "Whose but Yours were the words You dinned
into my ears through the voice of my mother, Your faithful servant? Not that at that time any of it sank into my heart to make
me do it. I still remember her anxiety and how earnestly she

urged upon me not to sin with woman. . . . Yet it was from You, though I did not know it and thought that You were silent and she speaking: whereas You were speaking to me through her." (II.3)

c. As might be expected from a man rich in human relationships, Augustine's references to God reveal a broad range of images, in addition to those linked with his mother. Augustine's God as reflected in the *Confessions*, ten years after his conversion, is a powerful, all-encompassing God: "O Thou, the greatest and the best, mightiest, almighty, most merciful and most just, utterly hidden and utterly present, most beautiful and most strong, abiding yet mysterious, suffering no change and changing all things: never new, never old . . . ever in action, ever at rest, gathering all things to Thee and needing none. . . . And with all this, what have I said, my God and my Life and my sacred Delight? What can anyone say when he speaks of Thee?" (I.4)

d. Augustine, like many people of faith, uses the language from human relationships. Sometimes that language is that of erotic love, sometimes that of an infant to a powerful parent God. Augustine's theology is too rich and complex to be limited in this way, but noteworthy images emerge. "Yet, Lord, I observed men praying to You: and I learnt to do likewise, thinking of You . . . as some great being who, though unseen, could hear and help me." "Hear my prayer, O Lord; Thou has drawn me out of all my most evil ways, that I should find more delight in Thee than in all the temptations I once ran after, and should love Thee more intensely, and lay hold upon Thy hand with all my heart's strength. . . ." (I.9 & 15)

e. The developmental change is noticeable in how Augustine addresses God. "As a boy I fell into the way of calling upon You, my Help and my Refuge; and in those prayers I broke the strings of my tongue—praying to You, small as I was but with no small energy, that I might not be beaten at school." (I.9) Augustine, as an adult aware of the divisions within himself, took as his task "to return to my self. I entered into my own depths, with You as guide; and I was able to do it because You were my helper. I entered, and with the eye of my soul, such as it was, I saw Your unchangeable Light shining over that same eye of my soul, over my mind. . . . Thou art my God, I sigh to Thee by day and by night. When I first knew Thee, Thou didst lift me up so that I might see that there was something to see, but that I was not yet the man to see it. . . . And I heard Thee, as one hears in the heart; and there was from that moment no ground of doubt in me. . . ." (V.10)

"This then is the fruit of my confession—the confession not of what I have been, but of what I am. . . . Thus I do it, in deed and in word, I do it under Your wings, for the peril would be too great were not my soul under Your wings and subject to You, and my infirmity known to You. I am but a little one, yet my Father lives forever and my Protector is sufficient for me. For He is the same who begot me and who watches over me: and You are all my good, You the almighty who are with me even before I am with You." (X.4)

Toward the end of the *Confessions* Augustine can calmly report his personal integration and inner peace: "Now my mind was free from the cares that had gnawed it, from aspiring and getting and weltering in filth and rubbing the scab of lust. And I talked with You as friends talk, my glory and my riches and my salvation, my Lord God." (IX.1)

f. His nine-year involvement with Manichaeism, whose ideology was that material things were evil, probably contributed to Augustine's feelings that sexual urges, which he felt so strongly, were evil. Augustine takes his own experience as paradigmatic for all human experience, and placed sexuality irremovably at the center of the human person.[124] His experiences psychologically colored his theology, to be sure, and in their impact on Western spirituality impacted the world of Therese centuries afterward in Lisieux.

St. Therese Martin (1873–1897)

In striking contrast to Augustine, Therese of Lisieux lived out her short life mostly in a small French town and Carmelite convent. Shortly after her death at the age of twenty-four, an extraordinary popular devotion grew up around her, mainly due to her piety which transcended the limits of the late nineteenth century French Catholicism in which she grew up. Her autobiography, *The Story of a Soul*, was written, under a formal order by her prioress, less than three years before she died. Her "little way" spirituality does not suit everyone, but for many seeking to live a life of faith she was an important spiritual model and guide. Therese's life and message tended to draw strong reactions, both positive and negative. There is no need here to be adoring or derogatory, but to see how the concrete events of her early life contributed to shaping her characteristic spirituality.

Both of Therese's parents, Louis and Zelie, had sought admission to religious communities but had been rejected. Zelie wed, by her own admission, only to produce souls for God's service. This wish was at first thwarted by her husband's initial desire to spend their marriage in sanctified celibacy. But Zelie's confessor managed to convince him otherwise.

Therese was born on January 2, 1873, the last of nine children, four of whom died. The young Therese was sickly, and when she was three months old she was sent to the home of a wet nurse for more than a year. She returned home where her four older sisters doted upon her, and she was the special favorite of her father, his "little Queen" (p. 41), upon whom he poured special attention. "God was pleased all through my life to surround me with *love*, and the first memories I have are stamped with smiles and the most tender caresses." (p.17)

Her "matchless mother" (p. 17) Zelie died from breast cancer in 1877 when Therese was four, and Marie, at seventeen, ran the household. The loss was difficult for Therese. "[M]y happy disposition completely changed after Mamma's death. I, once so full of life, became timid and retiring, sensitive to an excessive degree. One look was enough to reduce me to tears. . . ." (p. 35) Indeed the traumatic loss was such that even twenty years later she comments that "All the details of my Mother's illness are still present to me. . . ." (p. 33)

Therese's fifteen year old sister Pauline became for Therese her "Little Mamma." She was very close to Pauline: ". . . a bond was formed between our souls. You were my *ideal*; I wanted to be like you, and it was your example that drew me towards the Spouse of Virgins at the age of two." (p. 20) "When little Therese was sick . . . it isn't possible to explain the maternal tenderness she received. Pauline then made her sleep in her bed (incomparable favor) and gave her everything she wanted. . . . It was Pauline, too, who received all my intimate confidences and cleared up all my doubts." (p. 44) Nevertheless Therese called the ten years after her mother's death the "most sorrowful" period of her life, years of weariness and dissatisfaction.

At a young age she took on a demanding religious program of prayer, Mass, acts of charity and little sacrifices that she carefully toted up. When she was seven she began to make frequent sacramental confession, even though she did not receive First Communion, according to the custom of the time, until she was eleven years old.

During this period, she felt close and protected in her family. She describes, for example, a typical Sunday. "First, I stayed in *bed* longer than on the other days; then Pauline spoiled her little girl by bringing her some chocolate to drink while still in *bed* and then she dressed her up like a little Queen. Marie came to curl her hair. . . . Afterwards she was very happy to take the hand of her *King* who on that day kissed her more tenderly than usual. The whole family went off to Mass. All along the way to church and even in the church Papa's little Queen held his hand. Her place was by his side . . . everyone seemed to think it so wonderful to see such a *handsome* old man with such a *little daughter*. . . . This joyous day, passing all too quickly, had its tinge of *melancholy*. . . . I would begin thinking that the day of *rest* was coming to an end, that the morrow would bring with it the necessity of beginning life over again, we would have to go back to work, to learning lessons, etc., and my heart felt the *exile* of this earth. I longed for the everlasting repose of heaven, that never-ending *Sunday* of the *Fatherland!* . . . Then we all went upstairs to say our night prayers together and the little Queen was alone near her King, having only to look at him to see how the saints pray." (pp. 41–43)

Indeed, Therese was very close to her father. "Each afternoon I took a walk with Papa. We made our visit to the

Blessed Sacrament. . . . After the walk . . . we returned to the house; then I did my homework and the rest of the time I stayed in the garden with Papa, jumping around, etc., for I *didn't know* how to play with dolls. . . . I loved cultivating my little flowers in the garden Papa gave me. I amused myself, too, by setting up little altars in a niche in the middle of the wall. When I completed my work, I ran to Papa and dragged him over, telling him to close his eyes and not open them till I told him . . . then I'd cry out: 'Papa, open your eyes!' He would open them and then go into an ecstasy to please me, admiring what I believed was truly a masterpiece. . . . How could I possibly express the tenderness which *'Papa'* showered upon his Queen? . . . There were beautiful days for me, those days when my 'dear King' took me fishing with him. . . ." (pp. 36–37)

In October 1881 when she was eight and a half she began school at the Benedictine Convent school at Lisieux, but she was not happy there: "The five years I spent in school were the saddest in my life." (p. 53) Since so much of her life involved her religious practices, and because her shortness of breath precluded involvement in sports, "I didn't know how to play like other children and as a consequence wasn't a very pleasant companion." (p. 54) Her intelligence caused her to be placed in a class with girls older than herself and she did very well academically, but her five years at this school were very difficult for her. "I didn't know how to enter into games of my age-level; often during the recreations, I leaned against a tree and studied my companions at a distance, giving myself up to serious reflections!" (p. 81) "I succeeded very well in my studies, was almost always first, and my greatest successes were history and composition. All my teachers looked upon me as a very intelligent student. . . ." (p. 82) She confesses to some clumsiness, and bad handwriting. (p. 82)

She says that she loved being with children her own age but she seems to have had no skills in forming friendships. "I tried to make friends with little girls my own age, and especially with two of them. I loved them and they, in their turn, loved me insofar as they were *capable*. But alas! how *narrow* and *flighty* is the heart of creatures! Soon I saw my love was misunderstood. One of my friends was obliged to go back to her family and she returned to school a few months later. During her absence, I *had thought about her*, treasuring a little ring she had given me. When I saw my companion back again my joy was great, but all I received from her was a cold glance. My love was not understood. I felt this and I did not *beg* for an affection that was refused . . . not *knowing* how to win the good graces of creatures, I was unable to succeed. O blessed ignorance! which has helped me avoid great evils! How can I thank Jesus for making me find *'only bitterness in earth's friendships'!"* (pp. 82–83)

In 1882 when Therese was about nine, she experienced another loss which distressed her a great deal. Her "second Mother," her older sister Pauline, left the family to enter the Carmelite convent. Apparently no one helped the young Therese sufficiently to prepare for this second serious loss. She speaks of her anguish and heavy grief, "the sorrowful trial which broke little Therese's heart when Jesus took away her dear *Mamma*, her tenderly-loved *Pauline! . . .* Ah! how can I express the anguish of my heart! In one instant, I understood what life was; until then, I had never seen it so sad; but it appeared to me in all its reality, and I saw it was nothing but a continual suffering and separation. I shed bitter tears. . . ." (pp. 57–58)

Pauline tried to comfort her younger sister and explained life in the convent at Carmel. The convent was made up of cloistered nuns who sequestered themselves for prayer, work, and common life and monastic silence. Therese recalled that "I felt that Carmel was the *desert* where God wanted me to go also to hide myself. I felt this with so much force that there wasn't the least doubt in my heart; it was not the dream of a child led astray but the *certitude* of a divine call; I wanted to go to Carmel not for *Pauline's sake* but for *Jesus alone*." (p. 58)

Therese wanted to enter Carmel, but the prioress of the convent kindly told the little girl that "they didn't receive postulants at the age of *nine* and that I must wait till I was sixteen." (p. 59) Family visits to Pauline at Carmel were painful for Therese: "Ah! how I suffered. . . . I said in the depths of my heart: 'Pauline is lost to me!' " (p. 60)

Shortly after Pauline's entrance, Therese fell dangerously

ill. She could only understand the illness as a spiritual affliction unconnected to her psychological distress: "The sickness which overtook me certainly came from the demon; infuriated by [Pauline's] entrance into Carmel, he wanted to take revenge on me for the wrong our family was to do him in the future." (p. 60) "Towards the end of the year [1882], I began to have a constant headache. . . . It didn't cause me much suffering. I was able to pursue my studies and nobody was worried about me." (p. 60) She was allowed to visit Pauline on the day Pauline was to ceremoniously receive the habit. But on leaving Pauline at the end of the day she became very ill, and "the sickness became so grave that, according to human calculations, I wasn't to recover from it. I can't describe this strange sickness, but I'm now convinced it was the work of the devil. . . . I said and did things that were not in my mind. I appeared to be almost always delirious, saying things that had no meaning. . . . I often appeared to be in a faint, not making the slightest movement, and then I would have permitted anyone to do anything he wished, even to kill me, and yet I heard everything that was said around me. . . . I believe the devil had received an *external* power over me. . . ." (p. 62)

Therese suffered intensely from this nervous illness. She regarded the illness as the direct work of the devil enraged at Pauline's entry into Carmel and seems not to have understood how angry she herself was, an anger alien to her and uncharacteristic of herself. "[A] miracle was necessary for my cure . . . and it was Our Lady of Victories who worked it." (p. 65) Therese thought she saw a statue of the Virgin Mary smile at her during one of her nervous crises. The Virgin Mary then seemed to her like yet another mother and a more permanent one. "Finding no help on earth, poor little Therese had also turned towards the Mother of heaven, and prayed with all her heart that she take pity on her. All of a sudden the Blessed Virgin appeared *beautiful* to me, so *beautiful* that never had I seen anything so attractive. . . . At that instant, all my pain disappeared. . . ." (pp. 65–66)

With great joy Therese began the preparation for her First Communion. She joined other children in a preparatory retreat at school where they stayed at night. "The number of children was small, and it was easy to give each child particular attention, and certainly our teachers gave each of us their motherly care and attention. They spent more time with me than with the others, and each night the first mistress came, with her little lantern, and kissed me in my bed, showing me much affection. . . . I was not yet accustomed to taking care of myself. *Marie* was not there to comb and *curl* my hair, and so I was obliged to go and timidly offer my comb to the mistress in charge of the dressing rooms. She laughed at seeing a big girl of eleven not knowing how to take care of herself. . . ." (p. 75)

"The 'beautiful day of days' finally arrived! The *smallest details* of that heavenly day have left unspeakable memories in my soul! The joyous awakening at dawn, the *respectful* embraces of the teachers and our older companions! . . . Ah! how sweet was that first kiss of Jesus! It was a kiss of *love*; I *felt* that I *was loved*, and I said: 'I love You, and I give myself to You forever!' . . . for a long time now Jesus and poor little Therese *looked at* and understood each other. That day, it was no longer simply a *look*, it was a fusion; they were no longer two, Therese had vanished as a drop of water is lost in the immensity of the ocean. Jesus alone remained; He was the Master, the King." (p. 77)

"In the afternoon, it was I who made the Act of Consecration to the Blessed Virgin. It was only right that I *speak* in the name of my companions to my Mother in heaven, I who had been deprived at such an early age of my earthly Mother. I put all my heart into *speaking* to her, into consecrating myself to her as a child throwing itself into the arms of its mother. . . ." (p. 78)

After her confirmation, Therese was afflicted in May 1885 by "the terrible sickness of scruples" for a period of eighteen months. "All my most simple thoughts and actions became the cause of trouble for me. . . ." (p. 84) She fell ill again, and left school [in early spring, 1886] when she was thirteen and had private lessons several times a week with a tutor Mme. Papineau. Therese found this woman to be a "very good person, *very well educated* but a little old-maidish." (p. 85) Therese continued lessons with this tutor about a year and a half and then discontinued formal study when she was about fifteen. She had about as much formal school as the average girl in Normandy at that time.

During this period she used to visit the chapel and remain "before the Blessed Sacrament until the moment when Papa came to get me. This was my only consolation, for was not Jesus my *only Friend*? I knew how to speak only to Him; conversations with creatures, even pious conversations, fatigued my soul. I felt it was far more valuable to speak to God than to speak about him. . . ." (p. 87)

Therese, at this period, seems to have felt acutely alone and perhaps depressed. She used to be comforted by the thought of her family in heaven, an "eternal family reunion." (p. 88) When she was with her sister Celine, she could be happy and enjoy herself. Separated from Celine, she would be miserable and suffer headaches. (p. 89) Therese mentions a visit to an aunt, but because she was without one of her sisters she became so homesick that she had to be sent back home. As soon as she stepped inside the house, "my health returned." (p. 90)

When she learned of her sister Marie's intention of entering the Carmelite community, "I resolved to take no pleasure out of earth's attractions." (p. 90) The loss of this sister was grievous for Therese and caused her great sadness. She still was "very scrupulous" and in her sorrow prayed to her four dead siblings, "four angels" to have pity on "their poor little sister who was suffering on earth." (p 93) She continued to hold prayerful dialogues with "my little brothers and sisters . . . to speak with them about the sadness of our exile. . . ." (p. 93)

Therese found it hard, with Marie gone into the convent, to care for herself. "Being the youngest in the family, I wasn't accustomed to doing things for myself. Celine tidied up the room in which we slept, and I myself didn't do any housework whatsoever. After Marie's entrance into Carmel, it sometimes happened that I tried to make up the bed to please God, or else in the evening, when Celine was away, I'd bring in her plants. . . . If Celine was unfortunate enough not to seem happy or surprised because of these little services, I became unhappy and proved it by my tears. I was really unbearable because of my extreme touchiness; if I happened to cause anyone I loved some little trouble . . . I *cried* . . . and then when I began to cheer up, I'd begin *to cry again for having cried.*" (p. 97)

At Christmas, 1886, Therese heard her beloved father grumbling about still having to fill her shoes with gifts. Instead of showing how hurt she was by his criticism that she was too old for such attentions, she gathered her courage and acted as if she had not heard his remarks, and she managed to make this last childhood Christmas a happy time. This hiding of sacrifices with a smile was characteristic of her spirituality. She says that on that Christmas she received "the grace of leaving my childhood, in a word, the grace of my complete conversion." (p. 98)

Therese grew close to her sister. "Celine had become the confidante of my thoughts. . . . Jesus, wanting to have us advance together, formed bonds in our hearts stronger than blood. He made us become *spiritual sisters.* . . ." (p. 103) They shared spiritual conversations and Therese drew from the shared spiritual experiences a comparison with Augustine and his mother. "I don't know if I'm mistaken, but it seems to me the outpourings of our souls were similar to those of St. Monica with her son when, at the port of Ostia, they were lost in ecstasy at the sight of the Creator's marvels! It appears we were receiving graces like those granted to the great saints." (p. 104)

By the time she was fifteen she was intent on devoting her life to God and she asked her father to let her enter the Carmelite convent. With reluctance he agreed, although Carmelite rules stated that an individual could not join the contemplative community before the age of sixteen. With the support of her family, the determined Therese asked the prioress of the convent, the bishop of Bayeux and the pope himself for a special dispensation. Her request to the pope came during a pilgrimage she made to Rome with her father and sister. While journeying to Rome for the pilgrimage she prayed to "Our Lady of Victories to keep far from me everything that could tarnish my purity; I was fully aware that on a voyage such as this into Italy I could easily meet with things capable of troubling me. I was still unacquainted with evil and so was apprehensive about making its discovery." (p. 123)

Despite repeated and explicit injunctions from officials that no one should talk to the Holy Father, she called out to

Pope Leo XIII and even clung to his knees until she was pulled off by papal guards. Within a few months she was granted permission, and on April 9, 1888 she entered the Carmelite convent in Lisieux. She was fifteen years and three months. "I found the religious life to be *exactly* as I had imagined it. . . ." (p. 149) Others also found her to be a very spiritual and holy young person. A priest, Father Pichon, noted that her fervor was "childish," but was very affirming of her virtue. (p. 149)

The young Carmelite was very open with her superiors and spiritual directors. She had various names she applied to Jesus—that he was her [spiritual] "Director," and the "Spouse of Virgins," and she was "His fiancée." (pp. 155–158) The customs of the time, specifically the reception of the habit, tended to use wedding and espousal language, so Therese may have gotten her bridegroom references from these customs, for example, referring to herself as a "fiancée . . . adorned for her wedding day." (p. 158)

Because of some of the mental difficulties of her father (he had to enter a mental institution, the Bon Sauveur at Caen), Therese suffered very much. She was very concerned about her two sisters Leonie and Celine who were not members of Carmel. (pp. 155–156)

She began to develop a spirituality of small things and small deprivations. For example, "I was taken up, at this time, with a real attraction for objects that were both very ugly and the least convenient. So it was with joy that I saw myself deprived of a pretty *little jug* in our cell and supplied with another large one, *all chipped.*" (p. 159)

She began to experience considerable spiritual aridity but also times of great peace. When she pronounced her vows, "My union with Jesus was effected not in the midst of thunder and lightning, that is, in extraordinary graces, but in the bosom of a light breeze." (p. 166) Speaking of her vows and becoming the "spouse of Jesus," she tells how she was presenting "her *little* flower to the *little* Jesus. Everything was little that day except the graces and the peace I received." (p. 167)

At one point "I was having great interior trials of all kinds, even to the point of asking myself whether heaven really existed" (p. 173), but these experiences were also balanced by moments of great *"consolation and love."* (p. 174) "You know the rivers or rather the oceans of graces which flooded my soul. Ah! since that happy day, it seems to me that *Love* penetrates and surrounds me, that at each movement this *Merciful Love* renews me, purifying my soul. . . ." (p. 181) She refers to herself as "a little white flower." (p. 181)

Other times she speaks of "the desires of my poor *little soul"* and "my *little childish desires,"* but also feels the *"vocations* of the WARRIOR, THE PRIEST, THE APOSTLE, THE DOCTOR, THE MARTYR." [emphasis in original] (pp. 192–193)

During her nine years in the convent, she endured significant spiritual sufferings and aridity. (p. 165) In the last few years of her life she apparently enjoyed mystical experiences that included spiritual espousals, intense states of transforming union in which the soul achieves a sense of complete union with God. "I feel how powerless I am to express in human language the secrets of heaven, and after writing page upon page I find that I have not yet begun." (p. 189)

She also speaks of her inadequacies and child-like relationship with God. She calls herself a "child" (p. 196), "a little bird" seeking the Divine Sun (p. 199), behaving like "babies who when frightened bury their heads on their fathers' shoulders."

In the last two and a half years of her life under the urgings of her prioress she wrote her autobiographical *Story of a Soul,* reminiscences of childhood and her years in religious life. She portrays her mother and father as never saying a mean word and her sisters as thoroughly devoted to their parents and each other.

In 1896 she had her first experience of spitting up blood due to tuberculosis. She began to suffer serious difficulties in breathing, pains in her chest, swollen limbs. On September 30, 1897, at twenty-four years of age, she died of tuberculosis.

In less than thirty years, she was recognized as a saint of extraordinary holiness by the Catholic Church. On May 17, 1925 Pope Pius XI formally canonized Therese, saying that she achieved sanctity without going beyond the common order of things.

Reflections

Some reflection on Therese's account of her life can help illuminate the connection between some of the early psychological events of her life and the particular shape her spiritual journey took.

a. As for developmental issues, Therese suffered an extraordinary series of key losses during the early years of her life, during the pre-oedipal period, with traumatic consequences. First was her separation at three months from her mother to be put out with a wet nurse for a year. She was separated from this wet nurse and returned to her mother and family. Next was the loss of her mother through death, and then the loss of her mother-substitute, Pauline, caused her to be in grief: "[M]y happy disposition completely changed after Mamma's death." She understandably began to be fixed on issues of connection and dependence—at a pre-sexual level of development. The loss of her mother when Therese was four would have been during an important developmental period, a time of consolidating her self-representation and object representations. It is as if Therese partly got stuck at the stage of idealizing parental figures and responded with great stress at the loss of her sisters who entered the convent—losses which threatened her own independent well-being.

Therese seems to have been a gentle, affectionate child who endured these losses as genuine traumas. Indeed they probably played a role in some of her serious childhood illnesses, some of which seem to have been the result of holding back an understandable anger at her painful losses. She felt her anger, which would have seemed alien to her, as a demonic experience, and in a kind of psychological splitting the Blessed Virgin appeared as an idealized maternal figure "so *beautiful* that never had I seen anything so attractive. . . . At that instant, all my pain disappeared. . . ."

Her close-knit family had formed such a protective cocoon for Therese that nothing outside that ideal world could ever measure up to it. The timing of the losses in her life and the repeated nature of the same kind of loss of nurturing figures seem to have delayed Therese's maturing and intensified her dependent relationship on subsequent sisters. Part of her iron will in seeking entrance to Carmel proceeded from her strong wish and need to be in a safe place with her two older sisters Pauline and Marie. Obviously she knew the difference between human and divine love, but her spirituality has a child-like quality to it, a child unabashedly seeking the comfort of a parent. Carmel was where she would find a spiritual cocoon, a place of safety and a reunion with her sisters and a loving Divine Parent.

Her child-like quality comes out in some of her difficulties in forming relationships with her pre-teen and adolescent peers. She seems to have mistrusted friendships, and she had so much pleasure in being the doted-upon last child that she continued in a somewhat immature way being her Daddy's little queen and the doted-upon youngest sister. She related well with adults, but it regularly was as a charming, doted-upon younger child with a caring adult. This did change once she entered the convent, although she continued to feel warm and consoled when a confessor or superior spoke with praise or kindness toward her.

The early losses and her consequent depression-like grief possibly delayed the onset of sexual feelings and interests; later in her life we can notice some vague references to the sexual— a vagueness probably not surprising in the repressed and pious social environment of that time and place.

b. Concerning her God representations, it is not at all surprising that a key element in her relationship with God was a child-like quality that searched for a reassuring and caring presence—at times, an almost desperate search. Some of the qualities that she found in God, and in her devotion to the Blessed Mother, were a maternal presence, a comforting sense of security. The dominant images are of child to parent. "I put myself quickly in the arms of God and behaved like babies who when frightened bury their heads on their fathers' shoulders. . . ."

Her approach to God was characteristically more familial, that is, as a child more than as a lover. Although there are later references to God as "the Spouse of Virgins, the King of Heaven," her imagery is still that of a little girl, a child: "I was acting towards Him [God] like a *child* who believes everything is permitted." (p. 139) Even her references to Jesus seem more comfortable with images of the child Jesus than Jesus the Mystical Bridegroom, although she does make reference to this characteristic. She spoke to little children "about the eternal rewards that little Jesus would give in heaven to good little children...." (p. 112) Referring to profession as "the *beautiful day* of my wedding," she goes on to speak of becoming "the spouse of Jesus! It was the *little* Blessed Virgin, one day old, who was presenting her *little* flower to the *little* Jesus." (p. 167) She speaks of her cousin Jeanne's wedding and "how much I learned from her example concerning the delicate attentions a bride can bestow upon her bridegroom. I listened eagerly to what she was saying so that I would learn all I could since I didn't want to do less for my beloved Jesus." (p. 169) Her dominant psychological experiences were as a child receiving adults' attention, rather than as a young woman who dated and learned how men and women relate intimately as peers.

Her most comfortable role, accordingly, was to be a child. (cf. pp. 196–197) Even though she has a relationship with her "Beloved," often she returns to the idea of being the "little child," and a title she preferred was that of Sister Therese of the Child Jesus. "I had offered myself, for some time now, to the Child Jesus as His *little plaything*. I told Him not to use me as a valuable toy children are content to look at but dare not touch, but to use me like a little ball of no value which He could throw to the ground, push with His foot, *pierce*, leave in a corner, or press to His heart if it pleased Him; in a word, I want to *amuse little Jesus....*" (p. 136)

c. Later Maturing. When Therese was around the age of puberty, it is noteworthy that her spiritual relationship with Jesus intensified. She makes references to spiritual kisses, and the tone of her spiritual life—at times—is less focused on the person of God the Father and more on Jesus as Friend and Lover, and she speaks of her fusion with Jesus as "Master and King." (p. 77) She makes increasing references to the *Canticle of Canticles* and to the spiritual writings of St. John of the Cross (cf. p. 179) in which can be found more erotic metaphors for mystical union with God. Her writings from the last year of her life reveal a more adult quality in her relationship with God.

The traumas of early losses, while not damaging Therese's sense of self, enabled her to have permeable boundaries so that she related warmly with adults. She loved receiving the attention and affection of her father and her older sisters. She easily could experience the sense of union and closeness with a Divine Lover. Her early closeness with God, to repeat, was more like child with parent. Spiritual imagery that was more erotic is not dominant in her writings about her early life, and her special contribution was to express a child-like spirituality. References to spiritual kisses from Jesus tended to be more like a brotherly kiss than an adult lover's kiss, although later passages written shortly before her death reveal the intensity and strength of her spiritual feelings.

When she was in the convent, when she had some adult responsibilities for some of the novices, she seems to have been more psychologically mature in her relationships. She became more reticent about sharing her spiritual experiences. There were increasing periods of painful spiritual dryness, although she offers some hints of her relationship with God through the use of spousal imagery other saints and mystics used. At times her words burned with the mystical passion of closeness and love.

In spite of all, in spite of "joking by speaking like a child" (p. 252), and referring to herself as "a little bird" (p. 198), she had a good intellect and made shrewd observations about people and situations. Nevertheless she called her "understanding of the secrets of our Spouse" (p. 189) the "way of spiritual childhood." (p. vii)

d. Her conversion to an intense life of faith—very different from Augustine's—involved coming to terms with growing up, a yielding up of the pleasures of childhood. "It was December 25, 1886, that I received the grace of leaving my childhood, in a word, the grace of my complete conversion." (p. 98) Augustine's conversion was more of surrendering to God whose representation seems to have had some of the powerful characteristics of his mother.

e. Modern commentators on Therese are appreciative of her strengths. Therese's precocious piety can mask her very real struggles and toughness.[125] She had conflicts and she dealt with them with genuine control and self-abnegation. She would smile for the world and hide some of her real pain, reveling in her littleness.

In her own way, she had considerable powers of self-observation and evokes the closeness of her family—her articulateness of joy and fusion, closeness of being with sisters and father—natural extrapolation to the boundary-less relationship to Jesus—and comfortableness of fusion.

Conclusion

A balanced picture of Therese sees her efforts as grounded in very real human crises of signficant psychological pain. Her spirtuality was formed in a particular cultural context, one in which psychological insights were rudimentary; Freud was just a young physician with a brand new private practice when she died.

Comparison and Contrast

Both saints can be contrasted with regard to early family experiences, which include key relationships with parents, and how they viewed themselves in relation to God. Both Therese's and Augustine's God is tied up in how they think about themselves.

Both Augustine and Therese enjoyed special places in their families. Augustine was the pampered talented son, Therese the doted-upon last child. Therese suffered trauma while growing up that probably delayed for a time her development at a pre-oedipal level. Augustine, by contrast, grappled with overtly sexual feelings, while Therese contended with dependency feelings and concerns about emotional security. Therese is aware of never having sinned in any serious way (p. 149), while Augustine laments his sins, lusts and infirmities. Augustine's work makes frequent mention of his sexual feelings. For Therese sexuality was not a concern, with the exception of one brief reference to her pilgrimage to Italy as a fourteen year old: "I prayed Our Lady of Victories to keep far from me everything that could tarnish my purity; I was fully aware that on a voyage such as this into Italy I could easily meet with things capable of troubling me. I was still unacquainted with evil and so was apprehensive about making its discovery." (p. 123)

The origins of the psychological issues for both saints were quite different; Augustine's mother was too much present, while Therese's mother and mother-substitutes precipitously left her. The father of Augustine played a relatively minor role in the young Augustine's life, whereas Therese was very attached to her father.

The psychology and personality of both saints played a central role in their theology and spirituality. Sexual issues occupied a central place in Augustine's theology, with sex and original sin being the evil side of human beings, while the hallmark of Therese's spirituality is a pre-sexual child-like dependency and trust. It is impossible to imagine Augustine labeling his spirituality as one of spiritual childhood. And it is equally hard to imagine Therese, with her lack of educational opportunities and limited life experiences, doing battles with heretics and wanting to influence the course of Western Christianity— even though she yearned for martyrdom and wanted to be heroic in God's service. It is especially hard to imagine Therese lusting after all too human earthly lovers of which she had no experience.

Therese, in contrast to Augustine, suffered early trauma by losses, and so much of her spirituality has features of pre-oedipal dependence and attachment.

Augustine wrote his Confessions when he was at the height of his adult powers. He was very well educated by the standards of his time, and we would expect developmental differences between him and a relatively untrained person who spent her late teen years and early adulthood in a cloister. Therese was only in her twenties when she wrote. Her writing is more effective in evoking the joy of her childhood experiences. But she also can equally well convey her passion for God. The psychological point is that one's life experience and maturing experiences do shape and color the way a person experiences God and gives expression to that felt relationship.

Conclusion

Object relations theory contributes to the conversation between psychoanalysis and religion. The relationship got off on the wrong foot because Freud seemed to dismiss religion as an illusion or wish fulfillment which people must put behind themselves as they mature. In turn, religious writers defensively were reluctant to acknowledge those genuine insights of analytic thought into the psychological forces that impinged on religious behavior.

But conversations between religion and psychoanalysis have improved as post-Freudian psychoanalytic object relations theories articulated an interpersonal model of the human person. This model, which deals psychologically with the relationship with God, can cast light on the religious experiences of believers and can help us realize how thoroughly religious experience takes place in the context of human psychological life. The concreteness, even messiness, of human life and relationships shape and influence an individual's religious experience.

The task of this book has been to use some of these notions from object relations theory to illuminate and bring insight to several different areas of religious experience. The perspective here, to repeat, is a psychological view of the individual's relationship with God, as opposed to a theological view. The theme articulated is that an individual's early human relationships shape the individual's image of God and that the relationship with God needs to be seen in the context of a person's human development.

A cautious beginning has been made in empirical research, although this tends not to be the main strength of object relations or psychoanalytic theory. A small number of studies have investigated characteristics of an individual's parents and corresponding qualities in the image of God.[126]

Future research from an object relations point of view will likely be on some of the consequences of the object relations of individuals who have been psychologically or sexually abused and how this affects their relationship with God. Anecdotal evidence suggests, for example, that abuse from a male figure early in life will distort representations of a traditional male God. There is not, however, a direct correlation between characteristics of the abuser and the victim's images of God. Thus spiritual directors find that the victims of abuse have mixed experiences in their relationship with God, some rejecting any kind of God that is paternal or patriarchal because of their fear and hurt, while other adult victims have found solace in a God that is benevolent and idealized—the good "parent," as it were. Women who have been abused by men probably have some difficulty with images of a male God; they can continue to believe but may transform their images of God into a God that is nurturing and possessing more of traditionally feminine characteristics.[127]

Another area of further research is that psychologists have often overlooked the positive role that religion has played in the psychic economy of individuals. A healthy relationship with God can orient the individual positively in the universe and serve as an anchor in hard times. A healthy religion helps present the world as more benevolent and meaningful, as opposed to a scary world, a world of rage and fear, with no sources of hope or comfort. A religious stance such as this contributes to the maintenance of the self by helping to hold the self together and avoid psychological fragmentation.[128] In the face of the difficulties of life, a person's images of God and the person's relationship to God serve a crucial psychic function of assisting in providing for a coherent sense of self in a world of stress and conflict. Further, relationships with God and a community can help the individual move outside and beyond a self-centered view of the world and transcend the boundaries of the self.

This book hopes to have fostered a greater collaboration between psychology and theology. Perhaps more importantly readers may have gained insight into their own movements to-ward—and away from—God. After all, our knowledge of God is incomplete. As we learn about the mysteries of the human person, perhaps these insights can by analogy teach us more about the divine Mystery.

Notes

Introduction

1. Ana-Maria Rizzuto, "Afterword," in *Object Relations Theory and Religion: Clinical Applications* edited by Mark Finn and John Gartner (Westport, Conn. and London: Praeger, 1992), p. 156.

2. See Benjamin Beit-Hallahmi, "Between Religious Psychology and the Psychology of Religion," in *Object Relations Theory and Religion: Clinical Applications*, pp. 119–120.

3. Freud's thoughts on religion are complex and spread over a number of his writings. A few key texts are the following: *Standard Edition of the Complete Psychological Works: Totem and Taboo*, 1913 (Vol. 13), pp. 141–142, 147–148; *Ego and Id*, 1923 (Vol. 19), p. 37; "From the History of an Infantile Neurosis," 1918 (Vol. 17), pp. 115–117.

4. Ana-Maria Rizzuto, "Afterword," p. 157.

5. See Jay R. Greenberg and Stephen A. Mitchell, *Object Relations in Psychoanalytic Theory* (Cambridge, Mass. and London: Harvard University Press, 1983), p. 45.

6. W.W. Meissner, *Psychoanalysis and Religious Experience* (New Haven and London: Yale University Press, 1984), p. xii.

Chapter One. Object Relations Theory Applied to Religion: Issues and Controversies

7. These images are technically mental representations which have enduring existence as a mental organization that is constructed out of a multitude of impressions. An infant experiences many images of its mother, and by means of these gradually builds up a representation of the mother—an affective

mental structure. Cf. Joseph Sandler and Bernard Rosenblatt, "The Concept of the Representational World," *Psychoanalytic Study of the Child* (1962), Vol. 17, p. 133.

8. Otto Kernberg, *Object-Relations Theory and Clinical Psychoanalysis* (New York: Jason Aronson, 1976), pp. 56–58.

9. Sigmund Freud, "Project for a Scientific Psychology," *Standard Edition* (London: Hogarth Press, 1982), Vol. 1, p. 322.

10. Cf. Dale Boesky, "Introduction to Symposium on Object Relations," *Psychoanalytic Quarterly* (1980), pp. xlix, 48–50.

11. James W. Jones, *Psychoanalysis and Religion* (New Haven and London: Yale University Press, 1991), pp. 10–14.

12. Cf. Michael St. Clair, *Object Relations and Self Psychology: An Introduction* (Monterey, Calif.: Brooks/Cole, 1986), p. 3.

13. Cf. W.R.D. Fairbairn, "Endopsychic Structure Considered in Terms of Object-Relationships (1944)," in *Psychoanalytic Studies of the Personality* (London: Routledge and Kegan Paul, 1952), p. 84.

14. W.R.D. Fairbairn, "Object-Relationships and Dynamic Structure (1946)," in *Psychoanalytic Studies of the Personality*, p. 150.

15. Cf. W.W. Meissner, *Life and Faith: Psychological Perspectives on Religious Experience* (Washington, D.C.: Georgetown University Press, 1987), p. 27.

16. Cf. Ana-Maria Rizzuto, "The Father and the Child's Representation of God: A Developmental Approach," in *Father and Child: Developmental and Clinical Perspectives*, ed. by Stanley Cath, Alan Gurwitt and John Ross (Boston: Little, Brown and Co., 1982), p. 359.

17. Ana-Maria Rizzuto, *The Birth of the Living God: A Psychoanalytic Study* (Chicago and London: University of Chicago Press, 1979), and John McDargh, *Psychoanalytic Object Relations Theory and the Study of Religion* (Lanham, MD and London: University Press of America, 1983).

18. The work of scholars like Rizzuto and McDargh builds on, as might be expected, the early work of Freud. One of his

contributions is to turn upside down the understanding of Genesis 1:26–27, which tradition interprets as God creating humans in his own image and likeness. In a startling reversal Freud suggested that the opposite was true: that humankind "created God in our [image]" (*Psychopathology of Everyday Life*, 1901, p. 19). Freud apparently dismissed the reality of a separate personal God, and focused much of his energy in trying to understand how and why human beings create gods and demons. Essentially Freud locates the origins of God in defensive processes arising during the oedipal period. An important aspect is his relating ideas of God to exalted ideas of a human father in the flesh: the human father is exalted into the image of God. Because we have grown so accustomed to this insight it may have lost much of its dramatic impact. Freud sees the ultimate origin of religion in a childlike defense against helplessness: *Future of an Illusion*, 1927 (London: Hogarth Press, 1961/ 68), Vol. 21, pp. 17–18.

19. Ana-Maria Rizzuto, *Birth of the Living God*, p. 7.

20. W.W. Meissner, *Psychoanalysis and Religious Experience* (New Haven and London: Yale University Press, 1984), p. 141.

21. Ana-Maria Rizzuto, *Birth of the Living God*, pp. 10, 87.

22. Sigmund Freud, *Future of an Illusion*, 1927 (London: Hogarth Press, 1961/68), Vol. 21, p. 49.

23. D.W. Winnicott, *Playing and Reality* (New York: Basic Books, 1971), pp. 2 and 110.

24. Cf. James W. Jones, "The Relational Self: Contemporary Psychoanalysis Reconsiders Religion," *Journal of the American Academy of Religion* 59 (1991), p. 120.

25. Winnicott, p 14; cf. W.W. Meissner, "The Role of Transitional Conceptualization in Religious Thought," in *Psychoanalysis and Religion*, ed. by Joseph H. Smith and Susan A. Handelman (Baltimore and London: The Johns Hopkins University Press, 1990), p. 103.

26. Winnicott, pp. 3, 6 and 14.

27. Meissner, "The Role of Transitional Conceptualization," pp. 105, 106.

28. W.W. Meissner, "Psychoanalytic Aspects of Religious Experience," *Annual of Psychoanalysis* 6 (1978), p. 138.

29. Benjamin Beit-Hallahmi, "Between Religious Psychology and the Psychology of Religion," in *Object Relations Theory and Religion: Clinical Applications*, ed. by Mark Finn and John Gartner (Westport and London: Praeger, 1992), p 120.

30. Cf. Nathaniel Laor, "Psychoanalytic Neutrality toward Religious Experience," *Psychoanalytic Study of the Child* (1989) 44, pp. 211–230.

31. Rizzuto, *Birth of the Living God*, p. 4.

32. Rizzuto, *Birth of the Living God*, p. 177; see also Benjamin Beit-Hallahmi, p. 126.

33. Cf. Rizzuto, "Afterword," pp. 156–157.

34. Harry Guntrip, "Religion in Relation to Personal Integration," *British Journal of Medical Psychology* (1969) 42, p. 325.

35. Harry Guntrip, *Schizoid Phenomena, Object Relations and the Self* (New York: International Universities Press, 1969), p. 324.

36. Harry Guntrip, *Personality Structure and Human Interaction* (New York: International Universities Press, 1961), p. 257.

37. Moshe Halevi Spero, *Religious Objects as Psychological Structures: A Critical Integration of Object Relations Theory, Psychotherapy, and Judaism* (Chicago and London: University of Chicago Press, 1992), pp. x and xiv.

38. Spero, p. 55.

39. Spero, pp. 79, 83, 85.

40. Stanley A. Leavy, "Reality in Religion and Psychoanalysis," in *Psychoanalysis and Religion*, Ed. by Joseph A. Smith and Susan A. Handelman (Baltimore and London: Johns Hopkins University Press, 1990), p. 54.

41. D.G. Attfield, "The Argument from Religious Experience," *Religious Studies* (1975) 11, pp. 335–343.

42. Beit-Hallahmi, p. 126. Beit-Hallahmi also correctly notes that this essentially does not contradict the classic view that religion makes tolerable the human helplessness. Cf. Freud, *Future of an Illusion*, p. 32.

43. *Personality Structure and Human Interaction* (New York: International Universities Press, 1961), p. 257.

44. Harry Guntrip, "Religion in Relation to Personal Integration," *British Journal of Medical Psychology* (1969), 42, pp. 323–324.

45. Cf. W.W. Meissner, "Notes on the Psychology of Faith," *Journal of Religion and Health* (1969) 8, p. 69.

46. Robert L. Randall, "The Legacy of Kohut for Religion and Psychology," *Journal of Religion and Health* (1984) 23, p. 107.

Chapter Two. The Internal Image of God

47. Ana-Maria Rizzuto, *The Birth of the Living God: A Psychoanalytic Study* (Chicago & London: University of Chicago Press, 1979), p. 88.

48. Ana-Maria Rizzuto, p. viii.

49. See Sigmund Freud, 1914, "Some Reflections on a School Boy Psychology," SE, Vol. 13, p. 243.

50. Ana-Maria Rizzuto, pp. 8–10.

51. Ana-Maria Rizzuto, p. 7.

52. Ana-Maria Rizzuto, pp. 41, 44.

53. Ana-Maria Rizzuto, pp. 44–45.

54. Ana-Maria Rizzuto, pp. 8, 10.

55. "The Deep Structure of Religious Representations," in *Object Relations Theory and Religion: Clinical Applications*, ed. by Mark Finn and John Gartner (Westport, Conn. and London: Praeger, 1992), p. 3.

56. Ana-Maria Rizzuto, pp. 47–49.

57. Ana-Maria Rizzuto, p. 200.

58. Ana-Maria Rizzuto, "Object Relations and the Formation of the Image of God," *British Journal of Medical Psychology* (1974) 47, p. 88, and Ana-Maria Rizzuto, *Birth of the Living God*, p. 91.

59. A summary of chapter 6 of *Birth of the Living God*, pp. 93–108.

60. Ana-Maria Rizzuto, *Birth of the Living God*, pp. 46–47.

61. Ana-Maria Rizzuto, "Afterword," *Object Relations Theory and Religion: Clinical Applications*, p. 165.

62. "Images of God: A Study of Psychoanalyzed Adults," in *Object Relations Theory and Religion: Clinical Applications*,

Chapter 9, pp. 129–140. Some other empirical studies are: Ian T. Birky and Samuel Ball, "Parental Trait Influence on God as an Object Representation," *The Journal of Psychology* (1988), 122, pp. 133–137; Daniel J. Heinrichs, "Our Father Which Art in Heaven: Parataxic Distortions in the Image of God," *Journal of Psychology and Theology* (1982), 10, pp. 120–129; Carl W. Roberts, "Imagining God: Who Is Created in Whose Image?" *Review of Religious Research* (1989), 30, pp. 375–384.

63. John McDargh, *Psychoanalytic Object Relations Theory and the Study of Religion* (Lanham, Md.: University Press of America, 1983), pp. xvi–xvii.

64. John McDargh, p. 104.

65. John McDargh, "The Deep Structure of Religious Representations," *Object Relations Theory and Religion*, p. 2.

66. John McDargh, *Psychoanalytic Object Relations Theory and the Study of Religion*, p. 6.

67. See Ana-Maria Rizzuto, "Afterword," p. 160.

68. "God-Representation as the Transformational Object," in *Object Relations Theory and Religion: Clinical Applications*, chapter 4, pp. 57–72.

Chapter Three. The Influence of Early Psychological Development on the Adult Experience of God

69. Religious experiences can also involve other situations and contexts, not least of which would be service to one's neighbor and involvement with the human community. Here the main aspect of religious experience will involve the relationship with God.

70. W.W. Meissner, *Psychoanalysis and Religious Experience* (New Haven and London: Yale University Press, 1984), pp. 150–158. An earlier version of the same material is W.W. Meissner, "Psychoanalytic Aspects of Religious Experience," *Annual of Psychoanalysis* 6 (1978), pp. 103–141.

71. W.W. Meissner, *Psychoanalysis and Religious Experience*, pp. x and 150. Cf. John Fitzgibbons, "Developmental Approaches to the Psychology of Religion," *Psychoanalytic Review* 74 (1987), p. 125.

72. W.W. Meissner, "Psychoanalytic Aspects of Religious Experience," *Annual of Psychoanalysis* 6 (1978), p. 136.

73. Cf. John McDargh, *Psychoanalytic Object Relations Theory and the Study of Religion* (Lanham, New York & London: University Press of America, 1983), pp. 117–134.

74. This is Erikson's idea of epigenetic phases of development; cf. Erik Erikson, *Identity and the Life Cycle* (New York: W.W. Norton, 1959).

75. W.W. Meissner, *Life and Faith: Psychological Perspectives on Religious Experience* (Washington, D.C.: Georgetown University Press, 1987), p. 28.

76. Cf. for example, D.W. Winnicott, "From Dependence to Independence in the Development of the Individual," *Maturational Processes and the Facilitating Environment* (New York: International Universities Press, 1963), pp. 83–99.

77. Ana-Maria Rizzuto, *Birth of the Living God* (Chicago: University of Chicago Press, 1979), pp. 90–91.

78. Ana-Maria Rizzuto, *Birth of the Living God*, p. 92

79. A fuller treatment of these stages can be found in Otto Kernberg, "Normal and Pathological Development," in *Object Relations Theory and Clinical Psychoanalysis* (New York: Jason Aronson, 1976), pp. 55–83. Meissner and Rizzuto have only loosely spelled out "stages" for development of the God representation, based on standard development sequences in psychoanalysis. It must further be emphasized that stages blend into each other and overlap and can even be repeated.

80. Margaret Mahler, Fred Pine, and Anni Bergman, *The Psychological Birth of the Human Infant* (New York: Basic Books, 1975), p. 8.

81. Melanie Klein was one of the first to attempt to articulate the infant's inner experience. See, for example, her "On the Theory of Anxiety and Guilt," *Envy and Gratitude and Other Works, 1946–1963* (New York: Delta Books, 1975), pp. 25–42.

82. Cf. Heinz Kohut, *Restoration of the Self* (New York: International Universities Press, 1977), p. 185; Heinz Kohut, *The Analysis of the Self* (New York: International Universities Press, 1971), p. 107. Kohut is primarily speaking in terms of the experience of the self rather than merely an imagistic representation of the self.

83. W.W. Meissner, *Psychoanalysis and Religious Experience*, p. 139; Ana-Maria Rizzuto, *Birth of the Living God*, p. 188.

84. Ana-Maria Rizzuto, "The Father and the Child's Representation of God: A Developmental Approach," in *Father and Child: Developmental and Clinical Perspectives*, ed. by Stanley Cath, Alan Gurwitt and John Ross (Boston: Little, Brown and Co., 1982), pp. 360, 368.

85. Rizzuto, "The Father and the Child's Representation of God," p. 371.

86. W.W. Meissner, *Psychoanalysis and Religious Experience*, p. 139; W.W. Meissner, "Psychoanalytic Aspects of Religious Experience," *Annual of Psychoanalysis* 1978, pp. 139–140.

87. W.W. Meissner, "Psychoanalytic Aspects of Religious Experience," p. 130.

88. Sigmund Freud, *Civilization and Its Discontents* (1930) (London: Hogarth Press, 1961), standard edition, Vol. 21, pp. 64, 72.

89. Mahler's stage of separation and individuation reaches completion between eighteen and thirty-six months, but these figures are approximate and not to be held too strictly because of overlapping lines of development. Because multiple lines of development are being telescoped here, there will be an even further blurring and overlapping of chronological times.

90. Ana-Maria Rizzuto, "The Father and the Child's Representation of God," p. 359.

91. Ana-Maria Rizzuto, "The Father and the Child's Representation of God," p. 376.

92. Ana-Maria Rizzuto, "Afterword," in *Object Relations Theory and Religion: Clinical Applications*, ed. by Mark Finn and John Gartner (Westport, Conn. and London: Praeger, 1992), p. 379.

93. W.W. Meissner, "Psychoanalytic Aspects of Religious Experience," p. 140.

94. W.W. Meissner, *Psychoanalysis and Religious Experience*, pp. 153–154; W.W. Meissner, "Psychoanalytic Aspects of Religious Experience," pp. 131–132.

95. Ana-Maria Rizzuto, "The Father and the Child's Representation of God," p. 377; W.W. Meissner, "Psychoanalytic Aspects of Religious Experience," p. 140.

96. Cf., for example, Elizabeth A. Johnson, *She Who Is: The Mystery of God in Feminist Theological Discourse* (New York: Crossroad, 1992).

97. Rizzuto gives the example of Fiorella whose God representation was primarily formed from her paternal representation.

98. Ana-Maria Rizzuto, "Afterword," p. 380, and Ana Maria Rizzuto, "The Father and the Child's Representation of God," p. 373.

99. Ana-Maria Rizzuto, "The Father and the Child's Representation of God," p. 379. Cf. also Moshe Halevi Spero, *Religious Objects as Psychological Structures: A Critical Integration of Object Relations Theory, Psychotherapy, and Judaism* (Chicago and London: University of Chicago Press, 1992), p. 73.

100. W.W. Meissner, "Psychoanalytic Aspects of Religious Experience," pp. 132–133; W.W. Meissner, *Psychoanalysis and Religious Experience*, pp. 154–155.

101. The cases are Wolf Man and Rat Man; Sigmund Freud, "From the History of an Infantile Neurosis (1918)," *Standard Edition of the Complete Psychological Works of Sigmund Freud* (London: Hogarth Press, 1955, 1968), Vol XVII, pp. 7–122; "Analysis of a Phobia in a Five-Year-Old Boy (1909)," *Standard Edition* (London: Hogarth Press, 1955, 1968), Vol. X, pp. 5–149.

102. Cf. Edith Jacobson, *The Self and the Object World* (New York: International Universities Press, 1964), p. 53.

103. Otto Kernberg, *Object Relations Theory*, p. 75.

104. W.W. Meissner, *Psychoanalysis and Religious Experience*, p. 140; W.W. Meissner, *Life and Faith*, p. 32.

105. W.W. Meissner, "Psychoanalytic Aspects of Religious Experience," p. 134; W.W. Meissner, *Psychoanalysis and Religious Experience*, pp. 155–156.

106. W.W. Meissner, *Psychoanalysis and Religious Experience*, pp. 156–157.

107. Ana-Maria Rizzuto, "Afterword," p. 381.

108. W.W. Meissner, *Psychoanalysis and Religious Experience*, p. 145.

109. Ana-Maria Rizzuto, *Birth of the Living God*, pp. 200–201.

110. W.W. Meissner, *Psychoanalysis and Religious Experience*, pp. 157–158; W.W. Meissner, "Psychoanalytic Aspects of Religious Experience," pp. 135–136.

111. W.W. Meissner, *Psychoanalysis and Religious Experience*, p. 157; W.W. Meissner, "Psychoanalytic Aspects of Religious Experience," p. 136.

112. W.W. Meissner, *Psychoanalysis and Religious Experience*, pp. 157–158.

113. W.W. Meissner, *Psychoanalysis and Religious Experience*, pp. 157–158.

114. Cf. Abraham Maslow, *Religions, Values, and Peak-Experiences* (Columbus, Ohio: Ohio University Press, 1964).

115. See, for example, Carol Gilligan, Nona P. Lyons, and Trudy J. Hanmer, editors, *Making Connections: The Relational Worlds of Adolescent Girls at Emma Willard School* (Cambridge: Harvard University Press, 1990), and Judith Jordan, et al., *Women's Growth in Connection: Writings from the Stone Center* (New York: Guilford Press, 1991).

116. See, for example, James Fowler, *Stages of Faith: The Psychology of Human Development and the Quest for Meaning* (New York: Harper and Row, 1981).

Chapter Four. Case Studies of Two Contrasting Saints

117. Quotations from *The Confessions* are from the English translation of F.J. Sheed, *The Confessions of St. Augustine* (New York: Sheed & Ward, 1948), and checked against the Latin text, *The Confessions of St. Augustine (S. Aureli Augustini Confessionum Libri Tredecim)*, ed. by John Gibb and William Montgomery (Cambridge University Press, 1927, and reprinted by Garland Publishing Co., 1980, New York and London).

118. Therese's account of her life and interior journey is actually a collection of three different manuscripts written during the last three years of her life in obedience to her superiors and was not intended by her for publication. "It is for *you alone* I

am writing the story of the *little flower* gathered by Jesus" (p. 15; emphasis in the original). All quotations are from *Story of a Soul: The Autobiography of St. Therese of Lisieux*, trans. by John Clarke (Washington, D.C.: Institute of Carmelite Studies Publications, 1972) as checked against Sainte Therese de L'Enfant-Jesus, *Histoire D'Une Ame* (Paris: Les Editions Du Cerf, 1985).

119. Charles Kligerman, "A Psychoanalytic Study of the Confessions of St. Augustine," *Journal of American Psychoanalytic Association* (1957) 5, p. 476.

120. See, for example, Charles Kligerman, "A Psychoanalytic Study of the Confessions of St. Augustine," *Journal of American Psychoanalytic Association* (1957) 5, pp. 469–484; Don Browning, "The Psychoanalytic Interpretation of St. Augustine's *Confessions*: An Assessment and New Probe," in *Psychoanalysis and Religion*, ed. by Joseph A. Smith and Susan A. Handelman (Baltimore and London: Johns Hopkins University Press, 1990), pp. 136–159; Andres G. Nino, "Restoration of the Self: A Therapeutic Paradigm from Augustine's *Confessions*," *Psychotherapy* (1990) 27, pp. 8–18; Volney Gay, "Augustine: The Reader as Selfobject," *Journal for the Scientific Study of Religion* (1986) 25, pp. 64–76; Don Capps, "Augustine as Narcissist," *Journal of the American Academy of Religion* (1985), 53 pp. 115–127; Paula Fredriksen, "Augustine and His Analysts: The Possibility of a Psychohistory," *Soundings* (1978), pp. 206–227.

121. See Nancy Chodorow, *The Reproduction of Mothering: Psychoanalysis and the Sociology of Gender* (Berkeley & London: University of California Press, 1978), pp. 77, 84.

122. Kligerman, p. 71.

123. The working assumption here is that Monica and her husband had a conventional relationship, with the mother performing the majority of child care for the young Augustine.

124. See Elaine Pagels, *Adam, Eve, and the Serpent* (New York: Random House, 1988), pp. 105–106.

125. Barbara Corrado Pope, "A Heroine Without Heroics: The Little Flower of Jesus and Her Times," *Church History* (1988), pp. 56, 59; see also Joann W. Conn, "Therese of Lisieux from a Feminist Perspective," *Spiritual Life* (1982) 28, pp. 233–239.

Conclusion

126. See, for example, Ian T. Birky and Samuel Ball, "Parental Trait Influence on God as an Object Representation." *The Journal of Psychology* (1988), 122, pp. 133–137; Daniel J. Heinrichs, "Our Father Which Art in Heaven: Parataxic Distortions in the Image of God," *Journal of Psychology and Theology* (1982), 10, pp. 120–129; Carl W. Roberts, "Imagining God: Who Is Created in Whose Image?" *Review of Religious Research* (1989), 30, pp. 375–384.

127. Some of these issues have been confronted by feminist theologians and psychologists; see, for example, Rosemary Radford Ruether, "The Western Religious Tradition and Violence against Women in the Home," in Joanne Carlson Brown and Carole R. Bohn, eds., *Christianity, Patriarchy, and Abuse: A Feminist Critique* (New York: The Pilgrim Press, 1989), pp. 31–41. See also Annie Imbens and Ineke Jonker, *Christianity and Incest*, trans. by Patricia McVay (Minneapolis: Fortress Press, 1992).

128. Robert L. Randall, "The Legacy of Kohut for Religion and Psychology," *Journal of Religion and Health* (1984) 23, p. 107; cf. also H. Guntrip, "Religion in Relation to Personal Integration," *British Journal of Medical Psychology* (1969), 42, p. 328.

Bibliography

Attfield, D. G. "The Argument from Religious Experience." *Religious Studies*, 1975, *11*, 335–343.

Beit-Hallahmi, Benjamin. "Between Religious Psychology and the Psychology of Religion," in *Object Relations Theory and Religion: Clinical Applications*. Edited by Mark Finn and John Gartner. Westport and London, Praeger, 1992, pp. 119–128.

Birky, Ian T. and Ball, Samuel. "Parental Trait Influence on God as an Object Representation." *The Journal of Psychology*, 1988, *122*, 133–137.

Browning, Don. "The Psychoanalytic Interpretation of St. Augustine's *Confessions*: An Assessment and New Probe," in *Psychoanalysis and Religion*. Edited by Joseph A. Smith and Susan A. Handelman. Baltimore and London, Johns Hopkins University Press, 1990, pp. 136–159.

Capps, Don. "Augustine as Narcissist." *Journal of the American Academy of Religion*, 1985, *53*, 115–127.

Conn, Joann W. "Therese of Lisieux from a Feminist Perspective." *Spiritual Life*, 1982, *28*, 233–239.

Fairbairn, W. R. D. "Endopsychic Structure Considered in Terms of Object-Relationships (1944)," in *Psychoanalytic Studies of the Personality*. London, Routledge and Kegan Paul, 1952, 82–132.

————. "Object-Relationships and Dynamic Structure (1946)," in *Psychoanalytic Studies of the Personality*. London, Routledge and Kegan Paul, 1952, 137–150.

Fowler, James. *Stages of Faith: The Psychology of Human Development and the Quest for Meaning*. New York, Harper and Row, 1981.

Fredriksen, Paula. "Augustine and His Analysts: The Possibility of a Psychohistory." *Soundings*, 1978, *61*, 206–227.

Freud, Sigmund. "Project for a Scientific Psychology (1895)," *Standard Edition*. London, Hogarth Press, 1953/1974, vol. 1, pp. 283–387.

————. "Instincts and Their Vicissitudes (1915)." *Standard Edition*. London, Hogarth Press, 1953/1974, vol. 14, pp. 117–140.

————. *Future of an Illusion* (1927), *Standard Edition*. London, Hogarth Press, 1953/1974, vol. 21, pp. 5–56.

————. *Civilization and Its Discontents* (1930). *Standard Edition*. London, Hogarth Press, 1953/1974, vol. 21, pp. 57–145.

Gay, Volney. "Augustine: The Reader as Selfobject." *Journal for the Scientific Study of Religion*, 1986, *25*, 64–76.

Greenberg, Jay R. and Mitchell, Stephen A. *Object Relations in Psychoanalytic Theory*. Cambridge, Mass., and London, Harvard University Press, 1983.

Guntrip, Harry. "Religion in Relation to Personal Integration." *British Journal of Medical Psychology*, 1969, *42*, 323–333.

————. *Personality Structure and Human Interaction*. New York, International Universities Press, 1961.

Heinrichs, Daniel J. "Our Father Which Art in Heaven: Parataxic Distortions in the Image of God." *Journal of Psychology and Theology*, 1982, *10*, 120–129.

Imbens, Annie and Jonker, Ineke. *Christianity and Incest.* Translated by Patricia McVay. Minneapolis, Fortress Press, 1992.

Johnson, Elizabeth A. *She Who Is: The Mystery of God in Feminist Theological Discourse.* New York, Crossroad, 1992.

Jones, James W. *Psychoanalysis and Religion.* New Haven and London, Yale University Press, 1991.

————. "The Relational Self: Contemporary Psychoanalysis Reconsiders Religion." *Journal of the American Academy of Religion*, 1991, 59, 119–135.

Jordan, Judith V., Kaplan, Alexandra G., Miller, Jean Baker, Stiver, Irene P., Surrey, Janet L. (editors). *Women's Growth in Connection: Writings from the Stone Center.* New York, Guilford Press, 1991.

Kernberg, Otto. *Object-Relations Theory and Clinical Psychoanalysis.* New York, Jason Aronson, 1976.

Kligerman, Charles. "A Psychoanalytic Study of the Confessions of St. Augustine." *Journal of American Psychoanalytic Association*, 1957, 5, 469–484.

Laor, Nathaniel. "Psychoanalytic Neutrality toward Religious Experience." *Psychoanalytic Studies of the Child*, 1989, 44, 211–230.

Leavy, Stanley A. "Reality in Religion and Psychoanalysis," in *Psychoanalysis and Religion.* Edited by Joseph A. Smith and Susan A. Handelman. Baltimore and London, Johns Hopkins University Press, 1990, pp. 43–55.

McDargh, John. *Psychoanalytic Object Relations Theory and the Study of Religion.* Lanham, Maryland, and London, University Press of America, 1983.

————. "The Deep Structure of Religious Representations," in *Object Relations Theory and Religion: Clinical Applications.* Edited by Mark Finn and John Gartner. Westport, Conn. and London, Praeger, 1992, pp. 1–20.

————. "God, Mother and Me: An Object Relational Perspective on Religious Material." *Pastoral Psychology,* 1986, *34,* 251–263.

Meissner, W. W. *Life and Faith: Psychological Perspectives on Religious Experience.* Washington, D.C., Georgetown University Press, 1987.

————. "Notes on the Psychology of Faith." *Journal of Religion and Health,* 1969, *8,* 47–75.

————. *Psychoanalysis and Religious Experience.* New Haven and London, Yale University Press, 1984.

————. "The Role of Transitional Conceptualization in Religious Thought," in *Psychoanalysis and Religion.* Edited by Joseph H. Smith and Susan A. Handelman. Baltimore and London, The Johns Hopkins University Press, 1990, pp. 101–127.

————. "Psychoanalytic Aspects of Religious Experience." *Annual of Psychoanalysis,* 6, 1978, 103–141.

Nino, Andres G. "Restoration of the Self: A Therapeutic Paradigm from Augustine's *Confessions.*" *Psychotherapy,* 1990, *27,* 8–18.

Pope, Barbara Corrado. "A Heroine Without Heroics: The Little Flower of Jesus and Her Times." *Church History,* 1988, *57,* 46–60.

Randall, Robert L. "The Legacy of Kohut for Religion and Psychology." *Journal of Religion and Health*, 1984, 23, 106–114.

Ruether, Rosemary Radford. "The Western Religious Tradition and Violence against Women in the Home," in *Christianity, Patriarchy, and Abuse: A Feminist Critique*. Edited by Joanne Carlson Brown and Carole R. Bohn. New York, The Pilgrim Press, 1989, pp. 31–41.

Rizzuto, Ana-Maria. "The Father and the Child's Representation of God: A Developmental Approach," in *Father and Child: Developmental and Clinical Perspectives*. Edited by Stanley Cath, Alan Gurwitt and John Ross. Boston, Little, Brown and Co., 1982, pp. 357–381.

———. "Object Relations and the Formation of the Image of God." *British Journal of Medical Psychology*, 1974, 47, 83–99.

———. *The Birth of the Living God: A Psychoanalytic Study*. Chicago and London, University of Chicago Press, 1979.

———. "Afterword," *Object Relations Theory and Religion: Clinical Applications*. Edited by Mark Finn and John Gartner. Westport and London, Praeger, 1992, pp. 155–175.

Roberts, Carl W. "Imagining God: Who is Created in Whose Image?" *Review of Religious Research*, 1989, 30, 375–384.

St. Augustine. *The Confessions of St. Augustine*. Trans. by F. J. Sheed. New York, Sheed & Ward, 1948.

St. Clair, Michael. *Object Relations and Self Psychology: An Introduction*. Monterey, Calif., Brooks/Cole, 1986.

St. Therese of Lisieux, *Story of a Soul: The Autobiography of St. Therese of Lisieux*. Translated by John Clarke. Washington, D.C., Institute of Carmelite Studies Publications, 1972.

Sandler, Joseph and Rosenblatt, Bernard. "The Concept of the

Representational World." *Psychoanalytic Study of the Child,* 1962, *17,* 128–145.

Spero, Moshe Halevi. *Religious Objects as Psychological Structures: A Critical Integration of Object Relations Theory, Psychotherapy, and Judaism.* Chicago and London, University of Chicago Press, 1992.

Winnicott, D. W. *Playing and Reality.* New York, Basic Books, 1971.

Index